Business Letters For
Busy People

by

Jim Dugger

National Seminars Publications

6901 West 63rd Street P.O. Box 2949 • Shawnee Mission, KS 66201-1349
1-800-258-7246 1-913-432-7757

Business Letters for Busy People

Published by National Seminars Publications, Inc.

© 1991 National Seminars Publications, Inc.

Available to the trade exclusively from Career Press

Printed in the United States of America

1   2   3   4   5   6   7   8   9   10

ISBN 1-55852-059-7

PREFACE

Why do we call this a Business User's Manual? Because it's designed to be used, not just read. In a Business User's Manual, you not only get the easy-to-read impact of chapter by chapter "how to" information, but each section is also filled with checklists, ready-to-use letters and guidelines to help you do your job better, more effectively, more easily – right now! It's literally a user's manual for the business professional.

Business Letters for Busy People is written in the best-selling style of our desktop handbooks. That series has sold over a million copies because each book is packed with real-world ideas you can use. In this series, like the handbooks, we've packed the most concrete information, useful techniques and practical tips possible in the smallest space. So you don't have to wade through endless pages of fluff searching for that elusive kernel of wisdom.

The Business User's Manual series gives you concise, easy-to-use learning resources that get results. Check out the format and don't be surprised if you find yourself leafing through the pages for tidbits of fact and business trivia. The margins deliberately focus your attention, acting like a thumbnail index. And each chapter is tabbed on the margins, so you can turn right to the chapter you need to see. Read the chapters that are immediately important to you. Although there is a logic and order to the design of the book, you can read it in the order that best suits you. Each chapter stands alone.

We know you'll find this business User's Manual helpful. Read it, copy it and act on its advice. Reading a good book awakens our mind, but too often never gets carried into action; we close the book unchanged. But with this book, your reading becomes action. And action is the key to success.

Gary Weinberg
Vice President
National Seminars Publications

WHAT IS A
BUSINESS USER'S MANUAL?

It's a one-of-a-kind resource filled with practical tools, templates, checklists and guidelines designed to make your job easier. Features of the Business User's Manual include:

- Ready-to-use examples of commonly written letters

- Spiral bound for easy copying

- Concise, action-oriented explanations of key points and concepts

- Checklists and step-by-step guidelines to make writing easy

- Margin notes that draw your attention to important points

- Detailed index and appendices to answer specific questions about style, forms of address, etc.

- Tabbed margins to help you find what you need quickly

National Seminars Publications

Table of Contents

Chapter 1 — Writing From Scratch

You are busy no matter what your position. Since you are busy, you want to use your time as effectively as possible. The business letter takes time but can be written more quickly if you follow a few basic principles. (If you're in a hurry, skip to Chapters 4 – 9 for samples of the kinds of letters you need to write.) This chapter assumes you have a little free time to brush up on business letter writing.

Keep in mind these three points when you write a letter:

1. Business letters serve one purpose.
2. Business letters are expensive.
3. Business letters serve as a record.

Business letters serve one purpose. They are to communicate information. Countless hours are spent and too many letters are sent that say little or nothing. That's a waste of time for the sender and the receiver. Also, when the wages of the writer and the typist, along with the pro-rated cost of equipment and postage are figured in, business letters are expensive. It is important that they be cost-effective. Why write a business letter? Because business letters serve as a record. Letters are long-lasting, tangible evidence of information you communicate to others.

Four Considerations of a Business Letter

1. Subject
2. Audience
3. Purpose
4. Style/Organization

These are the four areas you must take into consideration for each business letter. If you do not, your letter will be ineffective.

Subject

Every piece of writing from the business letter to the novel revolves around a subject. Luckily, in the business world, the subject is usually specific and quite often supplied for you by someone else such as a boss or colleague, or demanded by a situation (firing, congratulatory letter, etc.).

It's a fact: the more specific your subject, the easier it is to write your letter.

For example, let's say that you need to request information about an order that did not arrive when it should have. If you are in charge of the account, writing the letter is easy. If you are not in charge of the account, it is harder for you to write the letter than the person who knows all the particulars. Regardless of the situation, stick to one or two subjects in your letter. Including more than two subjects clouds your message. Write another letter if you have more than two subjects.

Audience

This area is tricky because you may not know your audience. If you do, you can tailor your letter to that audience. Many times, however, your audience is larger than you expect. Your letter may be addressed to Terry Smith, but may be

In a study of 800 letters written by the top chief executive officers in the U.S., all 800 letters were found to be short, clear and personal. By the time they became CEOs, these people had learned never to send out a letter that didn't reflect those three basic principles of good writing.

read by several other people in that firm to receive the action you wish. If you are unsure of your audience, assume they are educated, reasonable people until you find out otherwise. Don't assume they have as much knowledge of the subject of your letter as you do or you may over-generalize or forget to include important details.

Purpose

Many letters are sent with a specific subject and audience in mind, but are not clear in their purpose.

Know why you are sending the letter. Is the letter to inform? Is it to request information? Is it to offer congratulations? Condolences? Is it to get the recipient to act on a request? All of these are very different purposes. You have probably received a letter that, after reading it, left you confused because you didn't know exactly what it said. The purpose was not clear.

Style/Organization

The first three areas dictate how you are going to write the letter.

1. Know WHAT you're writing about — SUBJECT
2. Know WHO you're writing for — AUDIENCE
3. Know WHY you're writing — PURPOSE

Now you are ready to be concerned with HOW you are going to write the letter. The first three areas can be determined in a matter of minutes if you are familiar with the ideas that need to be communicated. The fourth area takes more time. (If you're pressed for time, refer to the sample letters in Chapters 4-9.)

The "So What?" Test

When you have finished a draft of your letter, read each paragraph and ask yourself "So what?" in the same way a new reader might. If you can't answer that from the paragraph, consider leaving it out.

Organization

Most of this book is devoted to how different types of letters are organized. However, the basic organization for the body of a business letter is as follows:

Part 1 of Body	State your purpose.
Part 2 of Body	Explain what you want to happen or explain the information you have.
Part 3 of Body	Request action, conclude or thank the reader for his response.

Let's take a look at each of these parts. Notice these are parts or sections rather than paragraphs. In some cases, particularly Part 2, the parts may consist of more than one paragraph.

Part 1 of the Body

Get right to the point in the first sentence of the letter. When you read a novel, you expect to have background information before the story ever starts. When you read a business letter, you expect to be told immediately what will happen. Remember, your reader doesn't have any more time to wade through a long letter than you do.

This part is usually a short paragraph. Anything too long will cause the reader to lose patience.

Part 2 of the Body

This is the bread and butter of the letter. It explains the information you are giving, or it explains what you want the recipient to do. It doesn't need to be elaborate, but it does need to include all of the information that the recipient needs.

"Brevity is the soul of wit."

— William Shakespeare

If you have a lot of information, break it into short paragraphs or make a list. <u>Underlining essential information is one way to highlight key points for your reader.</u>

Your letter should be organized to help the recipient understand what he needs to know or what you want him to do.

Part 3 of the Body

"Tell 'em what you're going to say, say it, and tell 'em what you said."

This, like the first part, is usually a short paragraph. In writing classes, it's called the clincher. Not a bad way to remember its function. Depending on the purpose of your letter, it will do one of three things.

1. **Conclude.** In an informational letter, this allows you to point out the most important item or draw all your key points into one statement.

2. **Request action.** In letters that require a response, such as collection letters, you define the action you want the recipient to take. In this part, you tell him what he is to do and when he should do it. Do not be vague or you will get vague results.

3. **Thanks for response.** In some letters, this part is simply a thank-you for the recipient's attention, response or concern.

In many ways, the method of writing a business letter is like the rule of thumb for giving a speech: Tell them what you're going to talk about. Talk about it. Then tell them what you talked about.

The following sample letter shows how each of the three parts work:

State Your Purpose

Explain What You Want to Happen or Explain the Information You Have

Request Action, Conclude, Thank for Their Response

Capital Supplies
8995 Camden Rd., Williamsburg, WI 63094

October 2, 19XX

Lance Smith, Director
Terrance Trucking
P.O. Box 4440
Houston, TX 34598-4440

Dear Mr. Smith:

Fifteen of the last shipments we have made using your company have arrived damaged. We ask that you investigate the attached shipping orders and take the necessary action.

Since we have used your company for eight years with few problems, we feel that only one or two of the drivers may be negligent. All 15 shipments that arrived damaged were delivered either by Ted McCraken or Bob Smiley. In five of the shipments, our loading dock supervisor detected alcohol on the breath of Mr. McCraken. In four of the shipments, alcohol was detected on Mr. Smiley. I have attached our loading dock supervisors' reports.

Please review the attached documents. We wish to continue to use your firm but cannot if these two drivers are delivering to us. I shall expect a reply regarding your actions within two weeks of your receiving this letter.

Sincerely yours,

Carla Reginald
CLR:mjk
Enc. (10)

Style

Style is how you write the letter. Business letters used to be written in what might be called "businessese," a formal, stiff language. That is no longer true. The predominant style is matter-of-fact and conversational. Gone are such phrases as "the aforementioned" and "due to the fact that."

The Seven "C's" of Style

1. **Conversational.** Try to write the way you speak. Get rid of stilted phrases. Why say "due to the fact that" when you can say "because"? Would you normally say "the aforementioned information"? Why not, "the information" or, if you need to refer back to a point, "the previous information"?

2. **Clear.** The goal of clarity is that the reader understands precisely what you are saying. The language of your letter should be adapted to the recipient. This means that you write in a matter-of-fact, conversational tone. Use specific examples the reader can relate to. Don't assume that your reader understands the jargon of your trade. Remember, most letters will be read by people other than the recipient of the letter. These people may be unfamiliar with the technical language or jargon you use. Clarity also means organizing your letter so each paragraph deals with only one main idea, and presenting your ideas in a logical order. Your letter should not be a collection of random ideas. It should be single-minded in its purpose.

3. **Concise.** A concise letter eliminates all unnecessary words. Why use four words, "in as much as," when you can use one word, "because"? This is not to say that you can't write long letters, but the longer the letter, the more ineffective it becomes. It is better to write a short letter with attachments than a long, detailed one.

"Writing, when properly managed, is but a different name for conversation."

— Laurence Sterne

4. **Complete.** Make sure you have included all the information the reader needs to know. Don't include details that are interesting but not relevant. The biggest problem with leaving out information is that the reader has to make assumptions. For example, don't say, "When we last spoke about the situation," when you can say, "When we spoke on June 8 about hiring a new administrative assistant."

Remember that the reader can't read your mind. He can only read your letter and guess at what you left out.

5. **Concrete.** Use specific terms that cannot be misunderstood. Don't say, "The large order that we requested has not arrived." Say, "The order for 10,000 basins that we requested on May 3, 19XX, has not arrived as of June 20."

Write about what people can see, touch, smell, taste or hear. In other words, make your language tangible. Make it concrete.

6. **Constructive.** Use words and phrases that set a positive tone. Constructive words are like smiling when you greet someone. They leave a good impression. Words such as "failure," "you neglected" and "error" tend to distance the recipient from the writer. Words such as "agreeable," "proud" and "success" help create a positive tone.

7. **Correct.** The last step in writing any business letter is to proofread it. You automatically check your image in a mirror before going out or meeting someone. The letter you send is your image on paper. If it is riddled with spelling and typographical errors, it will detract from what you are trying to get across. The reaction will be, "He can't spell," or "she doesn't know how to type."

If you have a secretary, don't assume your secretary knows how to spell or punctuate. Luckily, most do; but proof your own letters. Why? Because it is your name that is signed at the bottom of the page, not your secretary's. You will be the one that looks bad.

In a Nutshell

Writing a business letter need not be difficult as long as you remember that you are attempting to communicate with another business person just like yourself. If you incorporate Subject, Audience, Purpose and Style/Organization into your correspondence, you will be on the road to better business letter writing.

Chapter 2 — Parts of the Business Letter

There are many parts to the business letter, some required, some optional. This chapter will review those parts and their order. The parts of the business letter are as follows:

1. Letterhead or Heading
2. Date
3. File Number (optional)
4. Personal and Confidential (optional)
5. Inside Address
6. Attention Line (optional)
7. Salutation (optional)
8. Subject Line (optional)
9. Body of the Letter
10. Complimentary Close (optional)
11. Signature
12. Added Information (optional)
13. Postscripts (optional)
14. Mailing Instructions (optional)

Parts of the Business Letter

Letterhead

Most business letters originating from a firm are written on the firm's letterhead. If you are writing a personal business letter or your firm does not use letterhead, then you need to include your firm's address in the heading (see Chapter 3 for the various formats). When you are using a heading instead of letterhead, place the date on the first line and the address on the subsequent lines as follows:

September 9, 19XX
359 Longview Road
Mt. Vernon, IL 65676

Date

This should be the date the letter is written. (See Chapter 3 for placement in the various formats.)

File Number

On occasion, you may wish to include the file number of the project, case, order, etc. that the letter refers to. The file number should be physically separated from the date by two spaces and from the part that follows (Personal and Confidential or Inside Address) by two spaces.

Personal and Confidential

Use these words when the person to whom the letter is addressed is the only one to read the letter. Physically separate these words from the rest of the letter by two lines. To assure confidentiality, include the words "Personal and Confidential" on the envelope.

The standard dateline in the U.S. is month, day, year (March 15, 19XX).

In Europe, however, the most widely used format is day, month, year (15 March, 19XX).

2

Inside Address

This should include the name of the person you are writing, his title if available, the name of the firm and the firm's address.

Attention Line

This is used when you do not know the name of the person you are writing and the letter is addressed to the firm. For example, the attention line may say, "Attention: Head of Accounting." It may also be used when you know the name of the person you are writing but are unsure of his title. The attention line may say, "Attention: Customer Service," thus indicating to the person receiving the letter that the letter also needs to be routed to the Customer Service department. Another way of doing this is to use the attention line and send copies of the letter to the appropriate department.

People don't usually get upset if you don't address them by their proper salutation, but they notice and appreciate it when you do.

Salutation

The salutation is used in all formats (see Chapter 3) except the Simplified Letter and the Memo. The following are correct salutations used in American business letters:

1. Dear Sir:
2. Dear Madam: (may be followed by title such as Dear Madam Chairperson:)
3. Gentlemen:
4. Ladies:
5. Dear Mr. Bryan:
6. My Dear Mr. Bryan: (formal)
7. Ladies and Gentlemen:
8. To Whom It May Concern or TO WHOM IT MAY CONCERN:

Parts of the Business Letter

One of the problems you may run into is writing to a person with a name that is not gender specific; for example, the name Terry. The simplest solution in the salutation is to say, "Dear Terry Lucas." If you are addressing a group of people in general, such as the shipping department, do not assume that they are all male. The old "Gentlemen:" is not acceptable. "Ladies and Gentlemen," though lengthy, is preferred. The way around having to use a salutation where you are unsure of whom you are writing to is to use the Simplified Letter (See Chapter 3).

Unless you're aiming for the Nobel prize, you shouldn't worry about your writing talent. Writing good business documents is a craft, not an art. It requires skill, not talent, and you can learn skills.

Subject Line

The subject line is most commonly used in the Simplified Letter. It announces the subject of the letter.

Body of the Letter

This is where you make requests or are replying to someone. It is the main part of the business letter. (See Chapter 3 for the various body formats.)

Complimentary Close

This varies in formality and is found in all business letters with the exception of the Simplified and the Memo. (See Chapter 3 for its placement.) The following complimentary closes are in order of decreasing formality:

1. Very truly yours,
2. Yours very truly,
3. Sincerely yours,
4. Cordially,
5. Sincerely,

Signature

There should be four lines between the complimentary close (or the body in the Simplified Letter) and your typed name so there is room for your signature.

Additional Information

If needed, this consists of the sender's initials in capital letters followed by a colon followed by his typist's initials in small letters. You may also find the abbreviations "Enc." for enclosure and "cc:" for copies sent followed by the names of persons receiving the copies.

Post Scripts

Additional information that might have been placed in the letter but for some reason was not. Not often used.

Mailing Instructions

Used to give the reader deadlines or pertinent information on mailing a reply. As you look through the major formats in Chapter 3, it's obvious that many of the parts listed above are not typically used in routine business correspondence. However, it helps to be aware of them in case you need to use them.

Studies have shown that postscripts, particularly handwritten, are often the first thing read and the first thing remembered. Be careful, however, that what you put in a postscript isn't so important that it makes you look forgetful or careless.

Chapter 3 — Format of the Business Letter

Business letter formats have changed over the years. If you went to school prior to the 1970s, you probably learned one basic form of business letter now called the modified semi-block. It was the bane of every beginning typist because of its strict rules concerning spacing. Luckily, the movement in business has been to simplify and provide choices. Now you have a choice of six different forms, some extremely simple, others more complex. This chapter will review the various forms. The six forms of business letters most commonly used are:

1. Block
2. Modified Block
3. Modified Semi-block
4. Simplified
5. Hanging Indented
6. Memo

It is likely that your organization may prefer one form over another. In the following explanations, the assumption is that you will be using letterhead stationery. If you are writing a personal business letter without letterhead, place your address immediately below the date as in the following example:

August 3, 19XX
2578 Tarrymore Lane
Chicago, IL 66557

Format of the Business Letter

Block

The Block format is by far the simplest. Every part of the letter starts at the left margin with spaces between each part. It has a very professional look to it. The order for the parts of the letter are date, inside address, salutation, the body, complimentary close, signature and added information.

Letterhead

Date
(2-3 spaces)
Inside Address
(2-3 spaces)

Salutation
(2-3 spaces)
Body
(2 spaces)

Complimentary Close
(4 spaces)

Signature
(2-3 spaces)
Additional Information

Italics Unlimited
231 W. 40th Street • Camden, NJ 08618 • (623) 555-2678

August 10, 19XX

Terry Lancaster
Capital Supply
657 Minden Ct.
Des Moines, Iowa 54687

Dear Mr. Lancaster:

xxxxxxxxxxxxxxxxxxxxxxxxxxxxxxxxxxxxxxxxxxxxxxxxxxxxxxxx
xxxxxxxxxxxxxxxxxxxxxxxxxxxxxxxxxxxxxxxxxxxxxxxxxxxxxxxx
xxxxxxxxxxxxxxxxxxxxxxxxxxx

xxxxxxxxxxxxxxxxxxxxxxxxxxxxxxxxxxxxxxxxxxxxxxxxxxxxxxxx
xxxxxxxxxxxxxxxxxxxxxxxxxxxxxxxxxxxxxxxxxxxxxxxxxxxxxxxx
xxxxxxxxxxxxxxxxxxxxxxxxxxxxxxxxx

Sincerely,

Joan McAllister

JFM:eer

Modified Block

Like the Block, the Modified Block has the advantage of separating paragraphs so that each one stands out. The spacing between sections remains the same as in the Block. The signature and date are placed to the right, thus allowing them to stand out also. The complimentary close and the signature are aligned and placed near the center of the letter, two spaces below the last paragraph.

3

Italics Unlimited
231 W. 40th Street • Camden, NJ 08618 • (623)555-2678

                                        August 10, 19XX

Terry Lancaster
Capital Supply
657 Minden Ct.
Des Moines, Iowa 52804

Dear Mr. Lancaster:

xxxxxxxxxxxxxxxxxxxxxxxxxxxxxxxxxxxxxxxxxxxxxxxxxxxxxxxxxx
xxxxxxxxxxxxxxxxxxxxxxxxxxxxxxxxxxxxxxxxxxxxxxxxxxxxxxxxxx
xxxxxxxxxxxxxxxxxxxxxxxxxxxxxxxxxxxxxxxxxxxxxxxxxxxxxxxxxx
xxxxxxxxxxxxxxxxxxx

xxxxxxxxxxxxxxxxxxxxxxxxxxxxxxxxxxxxxxxxxxxxxxxxxxxxxxxxxx
xxxxxxxxxxxxxxxxxxxxxxxxxxxxxxxxxxxxxxxxxxxxxxxxxxxxxxxxxx
xxxxxxxxxxxxxxxxxxxxxxxxxxxxxxxxxxxxxxxxxxxxxxxxxxxxxxxxxx
xxxxxxxxxxxxxxxxxxxxxxxxxxxxxxx

                                        Sincerely,

                                        Joan McAllister

JFM:eer

Date
(move to right)

Complimentary Close
(move to right)

Signature
(move to right)

Format of the Business Letter

"I hate quotations. Tell me what you know."

— Ralph Waldo Emerson

Modified Semi-block

You will recognize the Modified Semi-block as the format most commonly taught as "the business letter." It is the same as the Modified Block except that the paragraphs are indented five spaces. All spacing remains the same.

(Indent paragraphs five spaces)

Complimentary Close
(move to right)

Signature
(move to right)

Italics Unlimited
231 W. 40th Street • Camden, NJ 08618 • (623) 555-2678

August 10, 19XX

Terry Lancaster
Capital Supply
657 Minden Ct.
Des Moines, Iowa 52804

Dear Mr. Lancaster:

xxxxxxxxxxxxxxxxxxxxxxxxxxxxxxxxxxxxxxxxxxxxxxxxxxx
xxxxxxxxxxxxxxxxxxxxxxxxxxxxxxxxxxxxxxxxxxxxxxxxxxx
xxxxxxxxxxxxxxxxxxxxxxxxxxxxxxx

xxxxxxxxxxxxxxxxxxxxxxxxxxxxxxxxxxxxxxxxxxxxxxxxxx
xxxxxxxxxxxxxxxxxxxxxxxxxxxxxxxxxxxxxxxxxxxxxxxxxx
xxxxxxxxxxxxxxxxxxxxxxxxxxxxxxxxxxxxxxxxxxxxxxxxxx
xxxxxxxxxxxxxxxxx

Sincerely,

Joan McAllister

JFM:eer

Simplified Letter

This is useful when you do not know the title of the person you are writing to, or when you are writing to a company, government agency or organization. It eliminates the courtesy titles (Mr., Mrs., Ms., Dr.), the salutations and the complimentary close. The focus of the letter is on the body and what is to be said. The spacing is the same as the block format.

3

Italics Unlimited
231 W. 40th Street • Camden, NJ 08618 • (623) 555-2678

August 10, 19XX

Terry Lancaster
Capital Supply
657 Minden Ct.
Des Moines, Iowa 52804

RE: PRINTING SUPPLIES

Subject of Letter

xxxxxxxxxxxxxxxxxxxxxxxxxxxxxxxxxxxxxxxxxxxxxxxxxxxxxxxxxxx
xxxxxxxxxxxxxxxxxxxxxxxx

xxxxxxxxxxxxxxxxxxxxxxxxxxxxxxxxxxxxxxxxxxxxxxxxxxxxxxx
xxxxxxxxxxxxxxxxxxxxxxxxxxxxxxxxxxxxxxxxxxxxxxxxxxxxxxx
xxxxxxxxxxxxxxxxxxxxxxxxxxxxxxxxxxxxxxxxxxxxxxxxxxxxx
xxxxxxxxxxxxxxxxxxxxxxxxxxxxxxxxxxxxxxxxxxxxxxxxxxxxxxx

Joan McAllister

JFM:eer

Signature

Format of the Business Letter

Hanging Indented Letter

On occasion you will see this form, but for all practical purposes it is seldom used. Its main advantage is that it calls attention to the body and each of the paragraphs. Spacing between the lines and sections is the same as in previous examples.

Italics Unlimited
231 W. 40th Street • Camden, NJ 08618 • (623) 555-2678

August 10, 19XX

Terry Lancaster
Capital Supply
657 Minden Ct.
Des Moines, Iowa 52804

Dear Mr. Lancaster:

xxxxxxxxxxxxxxxxxxxxxxxxxxxxxxxxxxxxxxxxxxxxxxxxxxxxx

xxxxxxxxxxxxxxxxxxxxxxxxxxxxxxxxxxxxxxxxxxxxxxxxxxxxx
xxxxxxxxxxxxxxxxxxxxxxxxxxxxxxxxxxxxxxxxx

xxxxxxxxxxxxxxxxxxxxxxxxxxxxxxxxxxxxxxxxxxxxxxxxxxxxx
xxxxxxxxxxxxxxxxxxxxxxxxxxxxxxxxxxxxxxxxxxxxxxxxxxxxx
xxxxxxxxxxxxxxxxxxxxxxxxxxxxxxxxxxxxxxxxxxxxxxxxxxxxx
xxxxxxxxxxxxxxxxxxxxxx

Sincerely,

Joan McAllister

JFM:eer

Memo

A sixth form of letter is the Memo. Though used primarily as an inter-office letter, it is occasionally used as a business letter format. At the top of the Memo is indicated the name(s) of the sender(s), the name(s) of the recipient(s), the date and the subject. The abbreviation "RE" is sometimes used instead of "Subject." This information is placed at the left margin. The body of the Memo is in block form. A signature and additional information are optional with the signature being placed near the center and the additional information at the left margin.

MEMORANDUM

To: Terry Lancaster
From: Joan McAllister
Date: August 10, 19XX
Re: Printing Supplies

xxxxxxxxxxxxxxxxxxxxxxxxxxxxxxxxxxxxxxxxxxxxxxxxxxxxxxxxxxxxx
xxxxxxxxxxxxxxxxxxxxxxxxx

xxxxxxxxxxxxxxxxxxxxxxxxxxxxxxxxxxxxxxxxxxxxxxxxxxxxxxxxxxxxx
xxxxxxxxxxxxxxxxxxxxxxxxxxxxxxxxxxxxxxxxx

xxxxxxxxxxxxxxxxxxxxxxxxxxxxxxxxxxxxxxxxxxxxxxxxxxxxxxxxxxxxx
xxxxxxxxxxxxxxxxxxxxxxxxxxxxxxxxxxxxxxxxxxxxxxxxxxxxxxxxxxxxx
xxxxxxxxxxxxxxx

                                        Joan McAllister

JFM:eer
cc: Ted Kapstein, Marsha Little

Memo Information

(2 - 3 spaces)

Body
(1 space between lines, 2 spaces between paragraphs)

(2 spaces)

Signature
(2 - 3 spaces)
Additional Information

Chapter 4 — Collection Letters

This chapter has sample collection letters you may have to write. The types of collection letters included are:

- Notification (p. 27)

- Reminder (p. 28)

- Inquiry (p. 29)

- Urgency (p. 30)

- Final Notice/Ultimatum (p. 31)

In this section, at the side of the page, you will find a brief explanation of each part of the letter. The first letter, on page 27, identifies each section of the letter. Subsequent letters identify only changes to the basic format.

Step-by-Step Instructions

The purpose of the collection letter is to get the customer to pay an overdue bill.

Step 1: The first part of the letter should state the amount owed, the due date and the date purchased.

Step 2: The second part of the letter should indicate the deadline for paying the bill and any penalties that may result. You may also wish to indicate your company's policy concerning late payments, grace periods, penalties, etc.

Step 3: The third part of the letter should indicate the consequences of not paying the bill. Initially, these may be merely penalties, but as the bill becomes more delinquent it may include warnings of ruined credit ratings or that the bill will be sent to a collection agency.

Note: At the end of this chapter is a checklist to use when you write collection letters.

"Creditors have better memories than debtors."

— Ben Franklin

Notification

This letter is to notify the recipient that the bill is overdue.

Western Wear
2212 Boot Hill Rd. • Cheyenne, WY 82430

July 5, 19XX

Ted Wilson
515 Ramey Ct.
Laramie, WY 82430

Dear Mr. Wilson:

On May 15, 19XX, you purchased $319.04 of merchandise from our store in Laramie. Your payment of $100 is now overdue.

In the credit agreement you signed, you agreed to pay off your bill in three payments. The first payment of $100 was due June 15, 19XX. Please remit this amount promptly.

Failure to pay on time may affect your ability to charge merchandise at our store. Thank you for your prompt attention.

Sincerely,

Mary West
Credit Manager

MJW:cjl

Date

Inside Address

Salutation

State the Situation

Indicate Deadline

Indicate Consequences

Complimentary Close

Signature

4

Reminder

This letter reminds the reader that the bill is overdue and the payment still hasn't been received

Remind Recipient of the Situation

Request and Indicate Deadline

Western Wear
2212 Boot Hill Rd. • Cheyenne, WY 82942

August 5, 19XX

Ted Wilson
515 Ramey Ct.
Laramie, WY 82244

Dear Mr. Wilson:

This is to remind you that both your first and second payments of $100 are now overdue. This $200 plus the balance of $119.04 is due on August 15.

In the credit agreement you signed, you agreed to pay off your bill in three payments. The first payment of $100 was due June 15, 19XX, the second of $100 on July 15, 19XX, and the final payment of $119.04 on August 15, 19XX. Please remit the full amount in 10 days.

Failure to pay on time will affect your ability to charge merchandise at our store. Thank you for your prompt attention.

Sincerely,

Mary West
Credit Manager

MJW:cjl

Inquiry

This letter inquires why the bill isn't being paid. It assumes that the bill is overdue.

Western Wear
2212 Boot Hill Rd., Cheyenne, WY 82412

September 5, 19XX

Ted Wilson
515 Ramey Ct.
Laramie, WY 82190

Dear Mr. Wilson:

Is there some reason you have not paid your bill of $319.04?

In the credit agreement you signed, you agreed to pay off your bill in three payments. Your total bill is now overdue. Please remit $319.04 within 10 days. If you have any questions, problems or disputes concerning this bill, please contact me at 800-555-9875.

Failure to remit the full amount may mean that your bill will be turned over to a collection agency. Thank you for your prompt attention.

Sincerely,

Mary West
Credit Manager

MJW:cjl

Inquire

Indicate Deadline

Indicate Consequences

Writing Collection Letters

Urgency

This letter stresses the urgency of the customer taking some kind of action on his bill.

State the Situation

Indicate Consequences

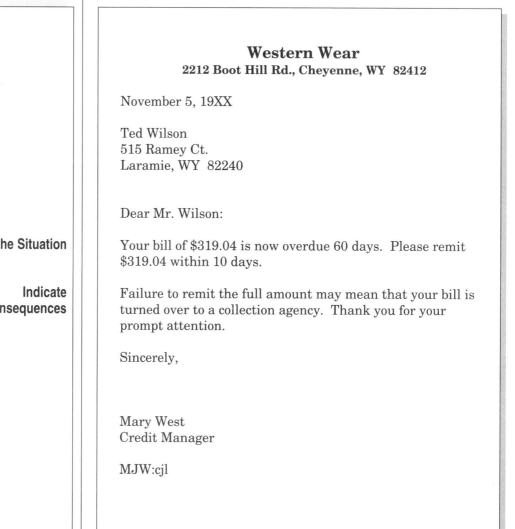

Western Wear
2212 Boot Hill Rd., Cheyenne, WY 82412

November 5, 19XX

Ted Wilson
515 Ramey Ct.
Laramie, WY 82240

Dear Mr. Wilson:

Your bill of $319.04 is now overdue 60 days. Please remit $319.04 within 10 days.

Failure to remit the full amount may mean that your bill is turned over to a collection agency. Thank you for your prompt attention.

Sincerely,

Mary West
Credit Manager

MJW:cjl

Final Notice/Ultimatum

This letter is the final notice the customer receives. It gives the customer an ultimatum, "If you do not respond, this will happen." After this letter there are no more chances.

Western Wear
2212 Boot Hill Rd., Cheyenne, WY 82412

November 5, 19XX

Ted Wilson
515 Ramey Ct.
Laramie, WY 82240

Dear Mr. Wilson:

Your bill of $319.04 is now overdue 90 days.

The total amount is due now. Please remit $319.04.

If your payment in full is not received by November 10, your file will be turned over to a collection agency.

Sincerely,

Mary West
Credit Manager

MJW:cjl

State the Situation

Indicate Deadline

Indicate Consequences

Writing Collection Letters

Checklist

_____ Was the tone of the letter firm but understanding?

_____ Did you state the amount owed?

_____ Did you state when the bill was due?

_____ Did you state the penalties, if any?

_____ Did you state the grace period, if any?

_____ Did you indicate the consequences of not paying the bill?

Chapter 5 — Sales and Promotion Letters

This chapter includes easy-to-use samples of sales and promotion letters. The broad categories are as follows:

- Request for Appointment (p. 35)

- Prospect Lead (p. 36)

- Letter of Introduction (p. 37)

- Follow-Up on Letter Sent (p. 38)

- Requesting Customer's Assistance (p. 39)

- Congratulations (p. 40)

- Sales Follow-Up (p. 41)

- Delinquent Reply (p. 42)

- Reminder a Sale Is About to End (p. 43)

- Announcing a Sales Campaign, Promotion or Incentive Program (p. 44)

- Acknowledging an Accomplishment (p. 45)

- Extremely Delinquent Reply (p. 46)

At the side of the page, you will find a brief explanation of each part of the letter. The first letter, on page 35, identifies each section of the letter. Subsequent letters identify only changes to the basic format.

Writing Sales and Promotion Letters

Step-by-Step Instructions

Sales and promotion letters are used by salespeople to set up or confirm appointments, announce sales promotions, congratulate salespeople on their successes and introduce new salespeople to their clients. The letter in and of itself is a sales tool.

Step 1: The first part of the letter states your purpose. Depending on the reason for writing the letter, this may vary from requesting an appointment to introducing a new salesperson.

Step 2: The second part of the letter gives details or background information. If you are making a request, then this part would give the reason for the request. For example, in a request for an appointment, the second part would set up the time for the appointment, the telephone number where you can be reached and the location of the appointment. If you are introducing a new salesperson, this part would give his background.

Step 3: The last part of the letter acts as a summary reminding the recipient of the letter's general nature. In many sales and promotion letters, this is a thank-you; in others it is a re-statement of what has been said previously. It may also be used to summarize the details of an appointment.

Note: At the end of this chapter is a checklist to use when you write a sales and promotion letter.

Request for Appointment

This letter is used by the salesperson to set up appointments and to announce his schedule. It is an introductory letter and should be followed up with another letter or phone call.

Carrington's
38 E. 91st., Chicago, IL 60614

January 25, 19XX

Linda Montgomery, Manager
A-1 Cleaners
2903 Burresh St.
Lincoln, NE 68506

Dear Ms. Montgomery:

I will be in Lincoln on February 3 and would like to meet with you at your office to discuss cleaning supplies that you may need in the second half of the year. I have enclosed our latest catalog.

I will contact you within 10 days to schedule an appointment. If you need to get in touch with me, my number is 800-555-9047. I look forward to meeting you. Thank you for your continued business.

Sincerely yours,

Douglas James
Sales Representative

DNJ:llr
Enc.

Date

Inside Address

Salutation

Request for the Appointment

Thank You and Confirmation

Complimentary Close

Signature

Additional Information

Sales and Promotion Letters

Prospect Lead

This letter is a follow-up from a lead given to the salesperson. It introduces the salesperson to the prospective lead.

State Your Purpose

Thank You and Request for Appointment

Tom's Sport Supply
665 Spinning Wheel Ct., Bilmont, UT 84106

December 4, 19XX

Terrance O'Toole
Golfers Teed Off
870 C. St.
Walla Walla, WA 98661

Dear Mr. O'Toole:

You and your firm have been recommended by Cal Gonzonles of Fore, Inc. Cal indicated that you may be interested in the line of products that we have, particularly our new Golflite line. I have enclosed our latest catalogue.

I will be in the Walla Walla area the week of December 16. I would like to meet with you and discuss how our Golflite line can help your business. I will contact you within the next 10 days to schedule an appointment. In the meantime, if you have any questions, my phone number is 1-800-555-1125. I look forward to meeting you.

Sincerely yours,

Chip Ashcroft
Sales Representative

CNA:pam
Enc.

Letter of Introduction

This letter is used to introduce one person to another —
such as a new salesperson to an established client.

Sea Lanes
8945 N.Shore Dr., Boston, MA 01611

November 22, 19XX

Carl N. White
Lobster Trappers Ltd.
Box 65
Kepaquadick Cove, ME 04103

Dear Carl:

I am happy to introduce you to our new sales representative,
Terry King. Mr. King will be in charge of servicing your
account.

Mr. King is a graduate of the University of Maine and holds
a degree in Sales and Marketing. For the last five years he
has worked as a salesman for Boston Fisheries and
Equipment. We are proud to have him on our staff and are
sure he will be able to give you the kind of service you have
come to expect from Sea Lanes.

Please call us if there is anything that we can do for you.
Mr. King will be contacting you within the next two weeks to
personally introduce himself, discuss his monthly schedule
and answer any questions you might have.

Sincerely yours,

T.K. (Tip) Walton
Director of Sales

TKW:joi

Introduce

**Background
Information**

Request

Sales and Promotion Letters

Follow-Up on Letter Sent

This letter asks the customer if he has received a letter.

Reference Previous Letter

Offer Assistance

Three W's
Box 231, Meford, Missouri 64506

December 1, 19XX

Caldonia Patterson
789 Winterwood Ln.
St. Joseph, MO 64503

Dear Ms. Patterson:

On November 10, I sent you a letter describing our newest product.

Did you receive the letter? I will be happy to answer any questions you may have and explain the unique features of this product and its benefits to you.

You are a valued customer and if there is any way that I can help you in making a decision, please feel free to call me at 1-800-555-1309.

Sincerely,

Kay Lynne Overmeyer
Sales Director

KLO:pst

Requesting Customer Assistance

This letter is used as a foot in the door and to request that a potential customer help the salesperson.

Martin Medical
3445 Medford Ave., Charleston, SC 29624

March 17, 19XX

Terrance Reilly
Box 557
Camden Creek, SC 29625

Dear Mr. Reilly:

I would like your help in solving a problem that people in businesses such as yours have.

Ask for Assistance

Each year businesses that sell medical supplies are faced with hundreds of new products. We would like your assistance in answering the enclosed survey. By doing so you will let us know how we can best serve you. I'll be calling you on Wednesday to ask your opinion concerning the survey.

Background Information

We value people like you who are willing to take their time to help us serve our customers better. Thanks for all your help.

Thank You

Sincerely yours,

Jack Larimer
Sales Manager 800-555-3590

JKL:jiw

Enc.

Congratulations

This is a goodwill letter on the part of the company or the salesperson to a client, and congratulates the client on an accomplishment.

Acknowledgment of Accomplishment

General Statement About Achievement

Capital Life Insurance Co.
369 Wilmington Blvd., Camden, NJ 07102

May 7, 19XX

Seth Tinkerton, Jr.
District Manager
839 Littleton Ct.
Morningside, NJ 07112

Dear Mr. Tinkerton:

Congratulations on being honored as the top district manager in Capital for March and April.

As you know, Capital Life honors its high achievers with our Call to Excellence Award. Your achievement in sales will be recognized at the June Convention in Philadelphia. We would like you and your agents to be our guests at a special banquet on June 5, 19XX, at 7:30 p.m. in the Cameo Room of the Hotel International during which you will receive the award.

Once again, congratulations. It is because of managers like you that Capital Life has achieved the success it has.

Sincerely yours,

John R. Liu
Vice President

JRL:cco

Sales Follow-Up

This letter is used to follow up on a sale that has been made. It may be a thank-you for the business, a clarification of the sale or a pitch for future sales.

Unlimited View
1854 Vision Ln., Arlington, TX 76016

February 15, 19XX

Marlene T. Thompson
Director of Sales
Omni-Optical Co.
334 S. 114th Ave.
Dallas, TX 75218

Dear Ms. Thompson:

Congratulations on your outstanding sales during our recent winter campaign. Omni-Optical sold 23 percent of our total volume during this program. Please commend your sales staff for their impressive efforts.

Because of your success, you now qualify for our quantity discount. Thanks again for your efforts. We look forward to sharing future sales successes with Omni-Optical.

Sincerely,

J. Kelly Bandman
Sales Representative

JKB:yek

5

Statement of Sales

Thank You

Delinquent Reply

This letter is used to remind a customer who has not responded to a recent letter.

Reminder

Review

Offer Assistance

Lakeland Insurance
7779 23rd St. E., Camden, NJ 08610

October 2, 19XX

Barry Wu
Wu's Gardens
558 Magnolia
Garden City, NJ 08638

Dear Mr. Wu:

Just a reminder that I recently sent you a computer printout of a proposal of health insurance for your employees.

Perhaps my letter was misplaced. I have attached another printout and hope that you will take the time to review it. As you can see, we offer a competitive package.

I will call you next Friday, once you have had time to review the proposal. I am anxious to do business with you. In the meantime, if you have any questions or concerns I can be reached at 308-555-9847.

Sincerely,

Terry Laforge
Sales Manager

TML:wie
Enc.

Reminder That a Sale Is About to End

This letter is used to remind a customer that a sale or sales campaign is about to end.

Myrna's Furniture Mart
709 Downey Rd., Wiltonshire, NH 03063

April 25, 19XX

Grant W. Werner
Rural Habitats
R.R. 3
Wiltonshire, NH 03104

Dear Mr. Werner:

It hardly seems possible but there is only one week left in our annual Eastertide Sale. Our letter announcing the sale four weeks ago seems like just yesterday.

It's still not too late to take advantage of this gigantic sale. The prices this last week are being slashed in half. I strongly urge you to come in and take a look at what we have to offer. Our entire sales staff is ready to work with you and Rural Habitats.

Attached is our Eastertide Sale flyer. Please take time to look it over and then come see us. You won't be sorry.

Sincerely,

Myrna L. Meyerhoff
Sales Manager

MLM:kwn
Enc.

Reminder

Review

Remind Again

Sales and Promotion Letters

Announcing a Sales Campaign, Promotion or Incentive Program

This type of letter informs clients of an upcoming sales promotion, incentive program or special sales packages that are available. It is followed by a personal call from the salesperson.

Unlimited View
1854 Vision Ln., Arlington, TX 76016

September 15, 19XX

Marlene T. Thompson
Director of Sales
Omni-Optical Co.
334 S. 114th Ave.
Dallas, TX 75218

Dear Ms. Thompson:

Announcement

Unlimited View will be starting our winter sales campaign on November 1.

Explain the Announcement

In the past, this campaign has enabled Omni-Optical to offer its customers a wide selection of products at very competitive prices. It is an outstanding way to attract new customers and build traffic for your business. I have enclosed a sheet explaining all of the particulars along with our latest catalogue.

Thank You and Deadline

I will call you within the next 10 days to answer any questions you have about the program and take your order. All orders have to be in by October 15. As always, it is a pleasure working with Omni-Optical.

Sincerely yours,

J. Kelly Bandman
Sales Representative

JKB:yek

Acknowledging an Accomplishment

Similar to the congratulatory letter, this letter acknowledges an accomplishment of a client, employee, relative of a client or employee, or friend of the company.

Pampered Prints
282 Kefauver Dr., Mt. Vernon, KY 42040

March 30, 19XX

Maria Fernandez
3333 Trenton Way
Mt. Vernon, KY 42049

Dear Maria:

Pampered Prints is proud that you are one of our employees. Your design for our Kute Kids line is outstanding.

Because of your design, Kute Kids is breaking all records in sales. During the first quarter, Kute Kids outsold all other lines in the Size 6-12 category. If this continues, you will be in line for promotion to Assistant Designer.

Keep up the good work. We need people like you, Maria, at Pampered Prints.

Sincerely yours,

Lily Marret
Director of Sales

LNM:ddl

Acknowledgement of Accomplishment

General Statement About Achievement

Re-congratulate

Extremely Delinquent Reply

This letter is used when a customer has not responded after a long period of time.

Statement of the Situation

Restate Original Letter

Cattleman's
3567 Hereford Ln., Tulsa, OK 73072

July 15, 19XX

J.M. Chesterman
900 Oilman Highway
Tinderbox, CO 80215

Dear Mr. Chesterman:

Yesterday I was going through our files and realized that we had never heard from you concerning our proposal to replace all of your cattle feeders.

I realize that four months have passed since I sent you the information, so I have attached our original proposal. I hope you will take time to look it over. We feel our prices are very competitive and the quality and durability of our feeders will actually save you money in the long term.

I will call you next Monday, once you have had time to review the proposal. I am anxious to do business with you. If you have any questions or concerns, I can be reached at 308-555-9847.

Sincerely,

Theodore "Tex" Miller
President

TJM:ssm

Enc.

Checklist

_____ Did you use a positive tone?

_____ Does the letter sell itself?

_____ Did you introduce the topic of the letter in the first part?

_____ Did you include all of the necessary details for the client such as date, time and place of appointment?

_____ Did you include a telephone number so that the client can reach you?

_____ Did you take the initiative in the letter for the action you desire?

_____ Did you include all background information or details necessary in the second part of the letter so the client understands the letter?

_____ Did you summarize, thank or re-congratulate in the last part of the letter?

_____ If you received the letter, would you do what you are asking the recipient to do?

5

6

Chapter 6 — Expressing Goodwill / Social Letters

This chapter has sample letters to help you write goodwill/
social letters. The broad categories are as follows:

- Appreciation (p. 51)
- Acknowledgment (p. 52)
- Official Anniversary (p. 53)
- Birthday (p. 54)
- Invitations — Formal (p. 55)
- Invitations — Informal (p. 56)
- Announcing Promotion — Personal (p. 57)
- Announcing Promotion — Public (p. 58)
- Encouragement (p. 59)
- Appointment to Office (p. 60)
- Birth of a Child (p. 61)
- Marriage (p. 62)
- Promotion (p. 63)
- Illness — Hospital (p. 64)
- Explaining Company's Policy and Position (p. 65)
- Recognizing a Suggestion (p. 66)
- Compliment (p. 67)
- Speech (p. 68)
- Congratulations (Social Letter) (p. 69)
- Apology (p. 70)
- Adjustment (p. 71)
- Appointment to a Committee (p. 72)
- New Employee (p. 73)
- Announcing New Fringe Benefits (p. 74)

At the side of the page, you will find a brief explanation of
each part of the letter. The first letter, on page 51, identifies
each section of the letter. Subsequent letters will identify
only changes to the basic format.

Expressing Goodwill / Social Letters

When asked what he thought about Western civilization, Mahatma Gandhi responded by saying, "I think it would be a very good idea."

Step-by-Step Guide

These letters are designed to promote goodwill among clients and employees.

Step 1: The first part of the letter states your purpose. Depending on the reason for writing the letter, this may vary from complimenting an employee on an accomplishment to apologizing for being unable to attend a social event.

Step 2: The second part of the letter gives the details or background information for the first part. This may be anything from explaining to a client the action that needs to be taken to correct a problem to giving details about a social event.

Step 3: The last part of the letter acts as a summary, reminding the recipient of the general nature of the letter. It may be a thank-you or it may restate what has been said in the first part of the letter. For example, if the letter is congratulatory, the last part recongratulates the recipient.

Note: At the end of this chapter is a checklist to use when you write a goodwill/social letter.

Appreciation

This letter expresses appreciation for something that was done. Quite often these are to employees of a company.

Seven Sisters
709 Starry Way, Council Bluffs, IA 50574

April 13, 19XX

R. K. Kirkman
4590 N. Iowa Ave.
Omaha, NE 68164

Dear Mr. Kirkman:

On behalf of the staff at Seven Sisters, I want to express my appreciation for your help in our recent ad campaign. Your tireless efforts made the campaign one of the most successful we have ever had.

Seven Sisters' success relies heavily on the commitment of its employees. Devotion such as yours allows us to be leaders in the field of fashion merchandising in the Omaha/ Council Bluffs area. Your efforts contribute to higher sales and these, as you know, mean increased profit-sharing for our employees.

Thank you for all of your hard work. Seven Sisters is successful because of employees like you.

Sincerely,

Laney Moore
President

LAM:rie

Date

Inside Address

6

Salutation

Reason for Appreciation

General Statement About the Company

Thank You

Complimentary Close

Signature

Additional Information

Acknowledgment

This letter expresses goodwill and acknowledges an accomplishment by someone who has a relationship to the company (employee, relative of an employee, friend of the company).

Acknowledge Accomplishment

General Statement About the Accomplishment

Re-acknowledge

KJZ, Inc.
45 Western Hills Rd., St. Paul, MN 55445

July 28, 19XX

Jake Tillis
R.R.1
Lake Woebegone, MN 56151

Dear Mr. Tillis:

KJZ is proud to have the new Twin Cities Corporate 10K Marathon winner on its staff. Your performance in Saturday's run was impressive.

It was most thrilling to see you cross the finish line wearing your KJZ t-shirt and then watch the performance again on the evening news. Your hard work and training have paid off. I was very proud to accept the corporate trophy as a result of your accomplishment.

The corporate trophy will be prominently displayed in the front lobby at KJZ. Thank you for representing us so ably.

Sincerely,

Kevin J. Zimmerman
President

KJZ: rmz

Official Anniversary

This letter recognizes an official anniversary such as the ordination of a priest or minister, when an elected official takes office or an employee's work anniversary.

6

Wood Hollow Cranberries
850 Random Rd., New London, CT 06320

April 8, 19XX

Edward Brown
8879 Kirksville Ct.
New London, CT 06320

Dear Ed:

All of us at Wood Hollow Cranberries wish to extend our sincerest congratulations on your tenth anniversary here at Wood Hollow. Your work, first as Assistant Plant Manager and now as Plant Manager, has been exemplary. We are most pleased to have you on our management team and look forward to many more years working with you.

Sincerely yours,

Grant Kleissman
President

GWK:gmn

Congratulations

Birthday

This letter is short and wishes someone (employee, relative of an employee, friend of the company, business associate) a happy birthday.

Birthday Wishes

Oglethorpe's and Osman
619 Leisure Blvd., Watchatee, FL 33873

May 25, 19XX

King Montgomery
774 Rising Hill Rd.
Lakeland, FL 32340

Dear King:

Is it that time of year again? Where has the time gone? Why, it was only yesterday that you were 26 and now you are turning 27. Hope your birthday is a happy one. We appreciate your work here at Oglethorpe's and Osman and hope that we enjoy many more birthdays together.

Sincerely,

Lawrence Oglethorpe
President

LJO:ccy

Invitations — Formal

This letter's formal language reflects the formality of the
event. It requires a formal reply.

Erskins and Co.
985 Washington, Boise, ID 83805

October 1, 19XX

Carmen and Ted Schmitt
800 Lander Ln.
Meridian, ID 83642

Dear Mr. and Mrs. Schmitt:

You are cordially invited to a formal dinner in honor of
Samuel Whitters on October 21, 19XX, 8 p.m. at the Boise
Hilton.

As you are an associate of Mr. Whitters, Mrs. Schmitt, we
would like you to speak briefly about his work in the lumber
industry. If this is possible, please let me know within the
next week.

Please note that this is a black-tie event. RSVP with the
names of those attending by October 14.

Sincerely yours,

John Randall, III
Chairman Social Committee

JKR:sat

**State Time, Place
and Event**

State Requirements

**Indicate Any
Deadlines**

Invitations — Informal

This letter is more informal and conversational in style. It may require a reply, but the reply may be verbal or informally written.

State Time, Place and Event

State Requirements

Indicate Any Deadlines

TeleWorld
1810 Ohio Ave., Little Rock, AR 72293

June 13, 19XX

Ramona Jenkins
55 Tremont
Little Rock, AR 72291

Dear Ramona:

The marketing department is having a *surprise* get-together next Thursday afternoon after work for the retirement of J.J. Small.

Please bring a gag gift to send J.J. on his way to a happy retirement. We're asking each person to contribute $5 for a legitimate retirement gift. Wanda Templeman is collecting.

Let Wanda know by Monday if you can make it so she can order enough refreshments.

Sincerely,

Chuck Meyers
Chairman, Social Committee

CJM:eem

Announcing a Promotion — Personal

This letter announces the promotion of an employee.

Nacadoces Notebooks
277 Linden, Nacadoces, TX 759363

August 1, 19XX

Truc Phan
3009 Clipclop Ln.
Nacadoces, TX 75963

Dear Mr. Phan:

After careful consideration, we are pleased to offer you the promotion to Vice-President in Charge of Sales.

Nacadoces Notebooks is offering this promotion to you because of your outstanding and untiring commitment to your work. Nacadoces Notebooks has grown substantially because of your efforts.

Congratulations. We're proud you are associated with us.

Sincerely,

Susanna M. Graham
President

SMG:eer

Announcement

The Reason

Welcome

6

Announcing a Promotion — Public

This memo announces the promotion of an employee to other members of the firm. In certain circumstances a letter may be used also.

Announcement

The Reason

Welcome

MEMORANDUM

To: All Employees
From: Susanna Graham, President
Re: Promotion to Vice President Sales
Date: August 5, 19XX

We are pleased to announce the promotion of Truc Phan to Vice President in Charge of Sales.

In the past 12 months, Mr. Phan has consistently provided outstanding service to his clients, brought in several new accounts and demonstrated outstanding sales leadership. Nacadoces Notebooks has grown substantially because of Mr. Phan's work. He will assume his new position on August 15 and will be located in Suite 25.

Please join me in congratulating Mr. Phan on his new position.

Encouragement

This letter offers encouragement to the employees of a firm.

RM Trucking
8092 Los Noches, Sante Fe, NM 87538

December 12, 19XX

Cappy Kappmeier
Wind Willow 13
Sante Fe, NM 87538

Dear Cappy:

Every year I take time to look forward to what the next year has in store for our employees. Next year's outlook is exciting.

RM Trucking in the past year has experienced phenomenal growth, moving from the tenth largest trucking firm in New Mexico to the second largest. We project that in the coming year we will become number one in New Mexico and number two in the combined states of New Mexico and Arizona. It is because of our farsighted staff that we have been able to achieve this kind of success. Naturally, this success affects everyone who works for RM Trucking. Because of our unique profit-sharing plan, each of you will benefit.

Next year will be exciting at RM for all of us involved. I hope you will make the most of these opportunities.

Sincerely,

Ronald Martin
President

RMM:wan

Statement of Purpose

Explanation of the Purpose

Restate Purpose

6

Appointment to Office

This letter congratulates the recipient on his appointment to an office in government or a charitable organization.

Congratulations

General Statement About Company

Re-congratulate (optional)

Clothier's International
793 W. Washington, Tanville, RI 02878

September 30, 19XX

Samuel R. Grant
1515 Sycamore Lane
Tanville, RI 02878

Dear Sam:

Congratulations on your recent appointment to the Tanville City Council. You should be proud of your accomplishment.

As you know, our policy of civic leave encourages our employees to participate in government. Your long-standing commitment to the community and this recent appointment make us proud to have you on our staff.

Keep up the good work. We need more people like you looking out for Tanville's interests.

Sincerely,

Lisa M. Mannerheim
Assistant Vice President

LMM:jjk

Birth of a Child

This letter congratulates the recipient on the birth of a child.

6

China Dolls For You
400 E. 60th St., Reno, NV 89502

June 4, 19XX

Lorraine R. Morris
55 Willow Bend Ct. #776
Reno, NV 89501

Dear Lorraine:

There is nothing more exciting than a new baby. We were all thrilled to hear about Travis's birth and know you are too.

Congratulations

All of us are looking forward to seeing you and Travis when you come to visit us next week. As you know, that's the time for our traditional "Shower of Gifts."

General Statement

Congratulations, Lorraine! You and T.K. have lots of reasons to be proud. Take care and remember, we're all envious of your new little one.

Re-congratulate
(optional)

Sincerely,

Shelli McAdam
Office Manager

SAM:kad

Marriage

This letter extends congratulations or best wishes when an employee or business associate gets married.

Congratulations

Re-congratulate
(optional)

Smith, Jones, and Yanacek
Counselors at Law
231 1st St. SE, Remington, MO 63302

February 22, 19XX

Linda Gleason
572 Westwood Apt. B
Remington, MO 63302

Dear Linda:

On behalf of Smith, Jones, and Yanacek, I would like to extend our best wishes on your marriage to Terry Gleason. We all wish you the happiest of times.

It is always a pleasure to share in the happiness of one of our employees. In your case, it was even more so, because you have been such an important part of our firm. I know I speak for all of us when I say that it couldn't have happened to a nicer person. We all look forward to your return after your honeymoon and hope that we will meet Terry soon.

Best wishes once again. We'll see you in a couple of weeks.

Sincerely,

Montgomery Smith
Senior Partner

MGS:gab

Promotion — Congratulations

This letter congratulates an employee or business associate on his promotion.

Cadrell's
290 26th Ave. Dr., Winston, GA 30067

August 8, 19XX

T. Molly Rathburn
8944 Tripp
Winston, GA 30067

Dear Molly:

I would like to congratulate you on your recent promotion to Assistant Plant Supervisor. You should be proud of your accomplishments.

Because of your hard work and dedication, you deserve this promotion. Employees like you help Cadrell's keep ahead of the competition and lead the way in the field of dental equipment. Your efforts are appreciated.

Congratulations again. Welcome to the management team at Cadrell's.

Sincerely yours,

J.K. Cadrell, Jr.
President

JKC:ltj

Congratulations

General Statement
(optional)

Re-congratulate

6

Illness — Hospital

This letter offers sympathy for an employee who is hospitalized.

Offer Sympathy

Additional Comments

Ft. Dodge Furnaces
445 Grand Ave., Ft. Dodge, IA 50501

Jan 10, 19XX

Carl Mattus-Wilson
319 Main
Manson, IA 50563

Dear Carl:

I was very sorry to hear that you have been hospitalized. I'm sure that the doctors at Trinity General will take good care of you and get you on your way.

Ft. Dodge Furnaces relies heavily on its employees and will feel your absence. I hope that you will recover quickly. We look forward to your return.

Sincerely,

Ole Munson
President

OHM:ijd

Explaining Company Policy and Position

This memo clarifies a company's policy and position for its employees. Normally a memo would suffice, but a formal letter may also be appropriate in certain circumstances.

MEMORANDUM

To: All Employees
From: Manuel Gonzales
Re: Policy Concerning Sick Leave
Date: December 23, 19XX

There seems to be some misunderstanding concerning Swithams' sick leave policy.

Statement of the Situation

Each employee is allowed 10 sick days per year during the first five years of employment. For five to 10 years of employment each employee is allowed 15 days of sick leave. Any employee of 10 or more years is granted 20 days of sick leave. Sick leave may be accumulated up to one full year (365 days). After an absence of two days an employee must seek medical advice and present a doctor's excuse upon return to work. Failure to do so will result in docking of pay for any sick leave after 2 consecutive days. For further information refer to the employee manual, page 23, or contact our Benefits Officer, Barbara Wieland.

Clarification

I hope this clears up any misunderstanding, particularly concerning the doctor's excuse.

Recognizing a Suggestion

This letter recognizes an employee or business associate for suggestions he has made.

Thanks

General Statement About Company (optional)

Re-thank (optional)

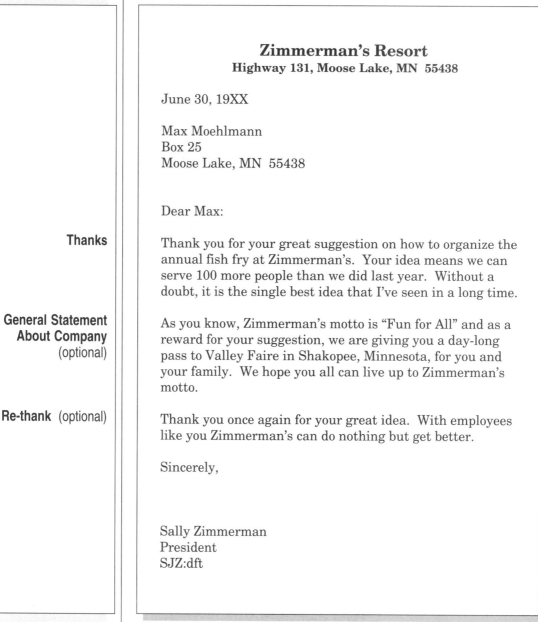

Zimmerman's Resort
Highway 131, Moose Lake, MN 55438

June 30, 19XX

Max Moehlmann
Box 25
Moose Lake, MN 55438

Dear Max:

Thank you for your great suggestion on how to organize the annual fish fry at Zimmerman's. Your idea means we can serve 100 more people than we did last year. Without a doubt, it is the single best idea that I've seen in a long time.

As you know, Zimmerman's motto is "Fun for All" and as a reward for your suggestion, we are giving you a day-long pass to Valley Faire in Shakopee, Minnesota, for you and your family. We hope you all can live up to Zimmerman's motto.

Thank you once again for your great idea. With employees like you Zimmerman's can do nothing but get better.

Sincerely,

Sally Zimmerman
President
SJZ:dft

Compliment

Similar to letters that congratulate and acknowledge accomplishments, this letter compliments someone (employee, relative of an employee, friend of the company) on something he has done.

Kids World
2255 Wilson Blvd., Galentine, IL 61036

January 20, 19XX

C.K. Leister
R.R. 5
Galentine, IL 61036

Dear C.K.:

I'd like to compliment you on your fine performance in the Galentine Community Theatre last Friday. You brought Stanley to life in *A Streetcar Named Desire*.

It is exciting for me to see fellow employees involved in the fine arts. I'm sure you are aware that Kids World has been a corporate supporter of the Galentine Community Theatre since its inception.

You are to be commended for your fine interpretation. Keep up the good work.

Sincerely,

Lorraine J. Black
President

LJB:kkc

Compliment

Relate to the Company (optional)

Re-compliment (optional)

Speech

This letter acknowledges a speech the recipient gave and comments on it.

Acknowledgment of Speech

Comments About the Speech

Re-acknowledgment

Coolidge High School
3222 25th St. N.E., Minot, ND 58504

May 23, 19XX

Barbara Rundle, Principal
Lake of the Woods High School
Box 66
Lake of the Woods, MN 20902

Dear Ms. Rundle:

I recently attended the North Central States Principals' Convention in Fargo and heard your speech on problems in the rural high school. I was most impressed and came away with many new ideas and insights.

I was particularly interested in your discussion of college preparation in the rural school. Although Calvin Coolidge High School does not qualify as a rural school, it has many of the same problems. An author I've found most enlightening who deals with rural schools is Garret Randolf. His works, *Rural America Who's Educating You?* and *One Room Schools Grown Up*, are both excellent. Are you aware of these titles? They weren't on your bibliography.

I shall look forward to your speech in Pierre as I see you are on the program.

Sincerely,

C. Max Hanks
Principal

CMH:bar

Congratulations (Social Letter)

This letter congratulates someone (employee, relative of an employee or friend of the company).

6

Linder Airplanes
515 Airport Rd., Waterloo, IA 50707

August 6, 19XX

Tommy Determan
Highway 20
Dunkerton, IA 50626

Dear Tommy:

Congratulations on winning the soap box derby during "My Waterloo Days." Your father, who works for us, couldn't stop talking about how proud he was of your victory.

I was interested in your win because I too was a soap box derby winner 21 years ago in Akron, Ohio. There's nothing quite like the thrill of knowing that something you've made is capable of winning.

Your dad is very proud of you. Congratulations once again and good luck at the Nationals!

Sincerely,

Charles M. Norris
President

CMN:cro

Congratulations

Personal Comments
(optional)

Re-congratulate
(optional)

Apology

This is a public apology. Such letters usually deal with social events.

Apologize

Personal Comments
(optional)

Re-apologize
(optional)

Trundle, Trundle and Smith
P.O. Box 2290, Frost, AZ 85603

December 1, 19XX

Warren and Marie Lambertson
4610 Country Club Way
Frost, AZ 85603

Dear Mr. and Mrs. Lambertson:

Please accept my apologies for missing your Thanksgiving brunch on November 23. I hope my last-minute change of plans did not inconvenience you too much.

As you know, I had planned on attending and was looking forward to it. However, my brother, who lives in Boston, Georgia, had emergency bypass surgery, and his wife asked me to be with her. Had that not happened, naturally I would have been with you.

Once again, I ask for your understanding in this matter and hope that my frantic, last-minute call to bow out was acceptable.

Sincerely yours,

Thomas J. Trundle, Sr.

TJT: mal

Adjustment

This letter requests an adjustment, either business or social, and asks for the understanding of the person for whom the adjustment is being asked.

Australian Outfitters
P.O. Box 212, Los Angeles, CA 99045-0212

October 3, 19XX

Corbin Reynolds
3510 Aroya Canyon Rd.
Hollywood Hills, CA 95234

Dear Mr. Reynolds,

I am sorry to inform you that your order of boomerangs will be delayed by four weeks because of a recent fire at Outback Boomerangs in Sydney, Australia.

Apologize

I hope this delay is acceptable. As soon as we found out, we contacted Woolabang Boomerangs in Alice Springs and were able to fill your order. Unfortunately, their boomerangs take longer to make because they are handmade. This is to your advantage because, though they are more expensive, we will absorb the difference in cost.

Excuse

Thank you for your understanding and cooperation in this unfortunate matter. If you have any questions, feel free to call me at 800-OUTBACK.

Re-apologize

Sincerely yours,

Tanner Dundee

TJD: mal

Appointment to a Committee

This letter congratulates an employee or business associate on an appointment to a committee.

Keystone Educational Agency
562 Rolling Hills, Birdsdale, PA 19508

January 10, 19XX

Karen Gorman
Box 67 R.R. 4
New Jerusalem, PA 18825

Dear Karen:

Congratulations

Congratulations on your appointment to the Excellence in Education Committee for Lucas County. We are pleased that one of our staff will be representing us and know that your experience and education will serve you well.

General Statement
(optional)

Striving for excellence in education in the tri-state area is of utmost importance. You have worked hard in the past supporting educational issues, and I'm sure you will continue your strong leadership role in the Excellence in Education Committee for Lucas County.

Re-congratulate
(optional)

If you need any help or resources, be sure to let us know. We are proud of your success and know that this appointment will bring you much personal satisfaction.

Sincerely,

Benjamin K. Douglas
Superintendent

BKD:ssp

New Employee

This letter welcomes a new employee to a business.

Pink's Shears, Inc.
763 Kekke Dr., Hibbing, MN 21111

May 6, 19XX

Linda Jean Tripp
1205 Mickey Mouse Dr.
Orlando, FL 32078

Dear Ms. Tripp:

It is my distinct pleasure to welcome you to Pink's Shears, Inc. We are looking forward to your arrival on May 21.

We at Pink's are very proud of our complete line of pinking shears and know that you will take the same pride in your work as we do in ours. Your role as Sales Director will be an important one. We know that with your education and experience you will bring to Pink's a much needed momentum.

Once again, welcome to Pink's. If there is any way I can help you make the transition let me know.

Sincerely,

Harold "Pinky" Pinkham
President

HJP:cpa

Welcome

General Comments

Re-welcome

6

73

Announcing New Fringe Benefits

This letter announces new fringe benefits to employees of a company.

Announcement

Explanation

Closing Statement

Warwick Manufacturing
1500 Burnside Parkway, Warwick, RI 02891

August 24, 19XX

Glenn Golden
90 Wuthering Heights Dr.
Kingston, RI 02881

Dear Mr. Golden:

It is my pleasure to announce that Warwick Manufacturing is offering a new employee benefit plan starting January 1.

After much discussion with management and labor we have settled on a plan that allows you to pick and choose those benefits you want and need. The enclosed brochure outlines the complete program. We are excited about it because you will have total control over your benefits.

We hope that you will be pleased with this new benefit package.

Sincerely,

Susanna M. Graham
President

SMG:eer

Checklist

_____ Did you use a pleasant tone in the letter?

_____ Did you state the purpose of the letter in the first part?

_____ Did you give background and details in the second part to further explain the first part?

_____ Did you summarize the letter in the last part?

_____ Is the letter sincere?

_____ Did you personalize the letter so that it doesn't sound institutional?

_____ Does the letter express goodwill?

_____ If you received the letter, would you feel good about it?

6

7

Chapter 7 — Community Activities Letters

This chapter has sample letters dealing with community activities. The broad categories are as follows:

At the side of the page, you will find a brief explanation of each part of the letter. The first letter, on page 79, identifies each section of the letter. Subsequent letters identify only changes to the basic format.

Community Activities Letters

Step-by-Step Guide

These letters address community activities that involve both individuals and corporations.

Step 1: The first part of the letter states your purpose. Depending on the reason for writing the letter, this may vary from asking a company to take part in a charity fund-raising drive to expressing appreciation for an employee's involvement in the community.

Step 2: The second part of the letter gives the details or background information for the first part. This may include giving a reason for declining a public office to indicating your company's policy about an employee's achievement.

Step 3: The last part of the letter acts as a summary reminding the recipient of the general nature of the letter. It may include deadlines, a thank-you, or a re-request.

Note: At the end of this chapter is a checklist to use when you write a community activities letter.

Solicitation of Funds

This letter requests that a company contribute to a charity.

JJT: Heavy Equipment
1288 E. U.S. 63, Sioux City, IA 50585

April 9, 19XX

William J. Buchheit
President
Sanders and Thoms
348 Lincolnway Dr.
South Sioux City, IA 50585

Dear Mr. Buchheit:

The United Benefit for Community Improvement is starting its annual drive this Monday. We hope you will contribute to this worthy cause.

In the past, Sanders and Thoms has been one of the leaders in the UBCI drive with its employees giving an average of 2.5% of their income to the fund. Naturally, they recognize that the fund improves their lives as well as the lives of others in the area. Additionally, I am sure we can count on your corporate support again. This year we are asking each corporation to match their employees' contributions.

I am sure you will want to continue your leadership in community development through your support of UBCI. We are asking that all contributions, employee and corporate, be in the UBCI office, 3001 Carrington Way, Sioux City, Iowa 56884, by May 15. Thank you for your continued support.

Sincerely yours,

Lannie Miller
Campaign Chairman

LJM:wit

Date

Inside Address

Salutation

Request

Indicate Support or Give Background Information

Re-request, Thanks and Deadlines

Complimentary Close

Signature

Additional Information

7

Acknowledgment of Contribution

This letter acknowledges that a company has contributed to a charity.

JJT: Heavy Equipment
1288 E. U.S. 63, Sioux City, IA 50585

April 25, 19XX

William J. Buchheit
President
Sanders and Thoms
348 Lincolnway Dr.
South Sioux City, IA 50585

Dear Mr. Buchheit:

Acknowledgement of the Contribution

The United Benefit for Community Improvement would like to thank you and your employees for your generous contribution to this year's fund drive. Your contribution of $99,751 is the largest corporate/employee contribution so far.

General Statement About the Contribution

I have instructed Donna Truemper, your UBCI chairperson, to let the employees of Sanders and Thoms know of their accomplishment. This year they gave an average of 2.75% of their income to the fund. Their contribution and yours will definitely help us meet our goal.

Re-acknowledgment

All of you at Sanders and Thoms are to be commended for your generosity. Thank you again for your contribution.

Sincerely yours,

Lannie Miller
Campaign Chairman

LJM:wit

Grant Request

Although most grant requests require a specific application form, you still need to send a cover letter with the form. This letter is a sample cover letter.

Salina Community College
45 Cottonwood Dr., Salina, KS 67401

October 14, 19XX

Cassandra L. Meyerhoff
Director of Grants
Salina Area Grant Office
350 1st St.
Salina, KS 67401

Dear Ms. Meyerhoff:

We would like to request a $15,000 grant for Salina Community College to improve access for the handicapped. I have enclosed our grant application.

The majority of the buildings on the Salina Community College campus were built prior to 1953. Those built after 1945 are accessible to the handicapped. Unfortunately, Atkinson Auditorium, where we hold graduation, monthly convocations and other major events was built in 1932 and is not accessible to the handicapped. The $15,000 grant would allow us to install ramps at each entrance and remove a row of seats for wheelchairs making the entire campus accessible to the handicapped.

Thank you for your prompt action on this grant. We shall look forward to hearing from you.

Sincerely yours,

Mary Ellen Feldman
Director of Physical Facilities

MEF:klo

Request for Grant

Background Information

Thank You

Refusal of a Request

This letter refuses a request made by another company or individual.

Marion Medical Supply
883 Union N.W., Marion, KY 41503

November 16, 19XX

M.D. Easton
Cranston County Republican Chairman
995 Rapid Run Rd.
Marion, KY 41503

Dear Mr. Easton:

Refusal

I regret that I will be unable to run for County Commissioner as we discussed last Friday. It is flattering to be asked, but circumstances do not allow me to run for office at this time.

Reason

I am declining because of prior commitments to my family and my business. I would not have the time to campaign or to devote to the position because of the prolonged illness of my mother and the amount of travel required by my business. I shall continue to actively support the Republican party both through volunteer efforts and monetary support.

Thank You for Understanding

Thank you for considering me. I appreciate your understanding.

Sincerely yours,

Duke Snow

DDS:van

Letter to Legislator Showing Support

This letter shows support of a bill being considered.

Mario's Pasta Inns, Inc.
803 King Ave., Odessa, TX 76514

September 8, 19XX

The Honorable Sarah Williams
Representative
Government Offices
9900 Ralston Way
Austin, TX 78603

Dear Ms. Williams:

I want to let you know that I support H.R. 305 which you recently introduced. Your continued concern for both restaurant owners and customers is admirable and H.R. 305 demonstrates that concern.

I own Mario's Pasta Inns, Inc., a chain of 15 Italian restaurants throughout Texas. Additionally, I am the past spokesperson for Restaurateurs International and am an active member of their governing board. We wholeheartedly support your bill that limits the sales tax on meals eaten out. We can see that raising the tax will hurt the owners and our customers.

Thank you for your concern and your untiring pursuit of keeping taxes in line. You have our support.

Sincerely yours,

Mario Napoli
President

MDN:klu

Statement of Support

Elaboration
(optional)

Thank You

7

Letter to Legislator Showing Concern

This letter shows concern over a bill being considered.

Statement of Concern

Elaboration (optional)

Restate Concern

Mario's Pasta Inns, Inc.
803 King Ave., Odessa, TX 79309

September 8, 19XX

The Honorable Hank Schlesselman
Representative
Government Offices
9900 Ralston Way
Austin, TX 45620

Dear Mr. Schlesselman:

I am most concerned about your support for H.R. 376. Its stringent restaurant sanitation requirements will double our costs which will, of course, be passed on to the customer. This may put many restaurants out of business.

I own Mario's Pasta Inns, Inc., a chain of 15 Italian restaurants throughout Texas. Additionally, I am the past spokesperson for Restaurateurs International and am an active member of their governing board. Our organization has thoroughly researched sanitation laws for restaurants throughout the world. Texas currently has the most stringent laws, and is recognized as a leader in the area of sanitation for restaurants. H.R. 376 in all cases has standards that even our medical labs would have trouble meeting.

I hope you will seriously consider the impact H.R. 376 would have on our economy. Such a bill can only cause the loss of jobs and income, and create disgruntled customers. Please withdraw your support of H.R. 376.

Sincerely yours,

Mario Napoli
President

MDN:klu

Expressions of Appreciation

This letter expresses appreciation for an act by an employee or a business associate.

Cranston Co. Republican Committee
995 Rapid Run Rd. Marion, KY 41503

October 30, 19XX

Duke Snow
Marion Medical Supply
883 Union N.W.
Marion, KY 41503

Dear Mr. Snow:

Thank you for your support in our recent election. Your hard work is greatly appreciated along with your monetary contributions.

When you indicated last November that you would not be able to run for commissioner, I was disappointed, but I knew that you would support us in whatever way possible. Once again, you came through. It is because of your untiring, behind-the-scenes work that we were able to sweep the election. You are essential to the Cranston County Republicans.

Thank you once again for all your hard work. Without you, we couldn't have done it.

Sincerely yours,

M.D. "Doc" Easton
Cranston County Republican Chair

MDE:klw

Express Appreciation

General Statement About the Situation

Re-express Appreciation

7

Thank You

Similar to the letter expressing appreciation, this letter thanks an employee or business associate for something they have done.

Thank You

General Comments

Re-thank

King's Court Auto
1500 Wright Way, Kitty Hawk, NC 27831

November 17, 19XX

Lee Kim Park
23 Timberline Dr.
Tarryton, NC 27789

Dear Mr. Park:

On behalf of the management at King's Court Auto, I would like to thank you for your recent participation in the United Way Campaign as Region 7's Unit Leader.

Your leadership in United Way not only helps the community but also reflects well on King's Court Auto. Civic participation is important, and we are proud of our employees when they take part in the community.

Thank you once again for all your hard work. Hats off to you!

Sincerely yours,

Donald King
Chairman of the Board

DSK:hey

Invitation to Serve

This letter invites someone with the company to serve on a committee or in a position — governmental or charitable.

Greater Pittsburgh Family Fund
760 Allegheny Dr., Mt. Lebanon, PA 16301

July 1, 19XX

Lucinda M. Grimschaw
993 White Water Way
Mt. Lebanon, PA 16301

Dear Ms. Grimschaw:

We of the Greater Pittsburgh Family Fund would like to invite you to chair the Health Committee for 19XX.

The Health Committee disburses funds to help families who have exhausted all other medical resources. We are asking you to chair this committee of eight people for one year. Presently, the committee meets weekly to review requests and act on them. Additionally, you would need to prepare a monthly disbursement report to be presented to the Greater Pittsburgh Family Fund's monthly Steering Committee. You would report directly to me.

Thank you for considering this offer. Please let me know by July 15, 19XX, if you are able to take this position. I look forward to working with you.

Sincerely yours,

Coretta Marshall
General Chairperson

CAM:tpw

Invitation

Explanation

Thank and Set Deadline

Invitation to Speak

This letter invites someone from the community to speak at a company related function.

Invitation

Explanation

Thank and Set Deadline for Reply

Enterprises, Ltd.
345 Waconia Rd., Denver, CO 80023

June 5, 19XX

Leonard Takamoto
5699 Mission Highway
Bismarck, ND 58578

Dear Mr. Takamoto:

We of Enterprises, Ltd. would like to ask you to speak at our Annual Stockholders' Meeting, August 10, 19XX, in Denver.

We wish to have you speak because of your reputation as an entrepreneur in the field of small businesses. As you may know, Enterprises, Ltd. acts as a clearing-house for small businesses and supplies ideas and seed money for new small businesses. Your recent article in *Success* speaks to the topic that we would like our stockholders to hear: "The Future of America Lies in Its Small Businesses." We hope you will consider this offer.

Thank you for your time. You will find attached a sheet outlining all of the particulars: remuneration, schedules, hotel and airline arrangements. Please let me know by June 15 if you will accept this speaking engagement. You can reach me at 208-555-7793.

Sincerely yours,

Hal J. Martinson
Executive Administrative Assistant

HJM:lld

Complimenting a Speaker

This letter compliments a speaker who has spoken at a company related function.

Enterprises, Ltd.
345 Waconia Rd., Denver, CO 80023

August 11, 19XX

Leonard Takamoto
5699 Mission Highway
Bismarck, ND 58578

Dear Mr. Takamoto:

On behalf of the stockholders of Enterprises, Ltd., I would like to thank you for your speech yesterday. Several stockholders have called me this morning to say how much they agreed with what you were talking about.

I was particularly pleased to hear that Enterprises, Ltd. is right on target with our mission statement concerning small businesses. The renewal of a solid economic base in the rural areas of the Midwest is the result of forward-looking people such as yourself and our board of directors. Dr. Michael Pearson, one of our largest stockholders, spoke to me this morning and put it succinctly, "Mr. Takamoto hit the nail on the head when he pointed out that the future is in small businesses."

Thank you for your inspiring speech. It was our privilege to hear you.

Sincerely yours,

Calvin R. Stiers
President

CRS:est

Compliment

Elaboration
(optional)

Recompliment and Thank

7

Checklist

_____ Did you state the purpose of the letter in the first part?

_____ Did you explain the purpose with details and background information in the second part of the letter?

_____ Did you summarize the purpose of the letter in the last part?

_____ Did you use a clear, informative tone?

_____ If the letter is one of appreciation or thanks, did you use a sincere tone?

Chapter 8 — Personal Business Letters

This chapter includes samples to help you write personal business letters. The broad categories are as follows:

At the side of the page, you will find a brief explanation of each part of the letter. The first letter, on page 93, identifies each section of the letter. Subsequent letters identify only changes to the basic format.

Step-by-Step

These letters are similar to goodwill/social letters. They are letters in which you, as a representative of the company, promote goodwill toward your employees, their relatives and business associates. They are also letters of recommendation and references.

Step 1: The first part of the letter states your purpose. Depending on the reason for writing the letter, this may vary from congratulating a business associate or employee to introducing the person you are recommending.

Step 2: The second part of the letter gives the details or background information for the first part. This may include details about an employee's accomplishments, background information about a character reference or recommendation, or personal comments concerning the first part.

Step 3: The last part of the letter acts as a summary, reminding the recipient of the general nature of the letter. It may include deadlines, a thank-you or a re-request. It is not necessary in many of the personal business letters to have a third part.

Note: At the end of this chapter is a checklist to use when you write a personal business letter.

Congratulations

This letter congratulates an employee, relative of an employee or business associate on an accomplishment.

Wilson and Company
1515 W. 23rd Ave., Tulsa, OK 74103

August 13, 19XX

Tim Ryan
3469 Campbell St.
Tulsa, OK 74103

Dear Tim:

Congratulations on your win in the Junior Division at the Tulsa Rodeo. Your mother has been telling everyone at work about how well you did.

To be able to win at such a young age is quite an accomplishment. I understand that not only did you win the Junior Division hands down, but also came within points of the Senior Division winner.

Your mom has a right to be proud of you. Congratulations once again!

Sincerely,

Karen R. Detweiler
President

KRD:cro

Date

Inside Address

Salutation

Congratulations

8

Personal Comments
(optional)

Re-congratulate
(optional)

Complimentary Close

Signature

Additional Information

Holiday Greetings

This short letter wishes an employee or business associate holiday greetings. This is particularly useful for those employees or business associates whose religion is not covered by the standard business greeting cards.

Goodwill Greeting

Gibralter Gems
112 Appian Way, Teasdale, WV 26656

December 15, 19XX

Joshua Schwartz
38 Fairview Ct.
Teasdale, WV 26656

Dear Josh:

The warmest of holiday greetings to you and your family. We at Gibralter Gems hope this holiday season brings you all of your wishes. Our regards to all of you.

Sincerely,

Thomas "Tip" Gibralter

TJG:ald

Thank You

This letter thanks someone (employee, relative of an employee, business associate) for something they have done.

Wobbly Horse Gift Shop
4866 Kilimanjaro Dr., Ann Arbor, MI 48897

April 3, 19XX

Robert Wu
300 Lister Ln.
Ann Arbor, MI 48898

Dear Mr. Wu:

I want to thank you for all the work you went through to send me the address and phone number of the gift shop in Hong Kong.

I called them this evening to ask about the tablecloths you told me about. You were right. They were most cordial and reasonable in their prices. I was able to order 10 tablecloths at a fraction of what they would have cost here in the States.

Thank you once again for your kind gesture.

Sincerely,

R. James Robinson

RJR:klr

Thank You

Explanation
(optional)

Re-thank

8

Inquiries

This letter asks for information to be used by the company.

Cat Man Dew Pet Suppliers
853 Regal Ave., Oklahoma City, OK 73009

February 14, 19XX

Pekka H. Huovienin
34 Raamintinuu
58 Helsinki 00580
Finland

Dear Mr. Huovienin:

Ask for Information

We are trying to locate information on a breed of cat called the Suomi Shorthair and understand that you are the leading expert on cats in Finland.

Explanation

We have a client who is interested in buying a Suomi Shorthair. She had seen one once at the New York Feline Show but has been unable to locate one since. She came to our shop and requested that we help her. Since the breed originated in Finland, we thought you might be able to give us some more information. We are most interested in the names of breeders that may have a kitten for sale.

Thank You and Deadline

We will call you within the next month to follow up on this inquiry. Thank you for all your trouble. We look forward to talking to you.

Sincerely,

Kathleen "Cat" Pence

KMP:nip

This letter requests an individual or company to act on the request.

PDQ Truckers
P.O. Box 2068, Denver, CO 80393-2068

August 21, 19XX

Cameron Mrstik
Mrstik's Mobile Station
582 Robinwood
Minihaha, MN 55437

Dear Mr. Mrstik:

Would you please return the black leather jacket that was left in your gas station last Saturday?

One of our truckers, Sam MacIntyre, left his leather jacket when he was on a run for us. Another of our truckers mentioned to Sam that he thought he saw a jacket just like Sam's hanging on your wall. He said it had to be Sam's as there are few leather jackets that say, "Ivydale, West Virginia," on them. Sam asked us to call you as he's on vacation in the Bahamas. We have tried repeatedly to reach you by phone, but your phone is always busy.

Please send the jacket as soon as possible, C.O.D. Thank you for your prompt response.

Sincerely,

Patrick D. Quentin
President

PDQ:msq

Request

Explanation

8

Thank You and Deadline

Refusal

This letter is an answer to the request letter and gives the reasons why the recipient won't act on the writer's request.

Refusal

Explanation

Mrstik's Mobile Station
582 Robinwood, Minihaha, MN 55437

August 25, 19XX

Patrick D. Quentin, President
PDQ Truckers
P.O. Box 2068
Denver, CO 80393-2068

Dear Mr. Quentin:

I would like to return Mr. MacIntyre's jacket to him, but I don't have it.

The jacket your trucker saw says, "I love Dale, Wes and Virginia." I had that jacket made specially for my wife. Those are our three children's names. I checked our register of truckers and there was no Sam MacIntyre at our station on the Saturday you mentioned. Perhaps he was at Mrs. Rick's Mobile Station on the interstate. People get us mixed up all the time.

I'm sorry I couldn't help you. I hope Mr. MacIntyre finds his jacket soon.

Sincerely,

Cameron Mrstik

CJM:mjm

Letters of Introduction

This letter introduces a person to a company or individual. Letters of introduction are similar to references, quite often describing the qualifications of the person to be introduced.

Campbell, Wilson, and Sons
472 Captain's Dr., Boston, MA 02031

October 7, 19XX

R. Hunter Wing
333 B. Ave. E.
Lincoln, NE 68530

Dear R. H.:

I would like to introduce you to James N. Glandorf who will be moving to Lincoln in November. As a fellow Pi Kappa Kappa, would you consider him for a position with your firm?

Mr. Glandorf worked in our law office during this last year. He was given the assignment of divorce cases which he handled extremely well and was well on his way to establishing himself as one of the best divorce lawyers I have ever seen. James was in line for a partnership here also but wanted to return to his native Nebraska, which I understand, being a Midwesterner myself. I have enclosed a reference from each of our partners. I'm sure you'll find that all of us held James in the highest regard.

Please take time to read the references and extend our greetings to James when he arrives. I have promised him nothing, but am sure that you will help him in any way that you would any other fellow Pi Kappa Kappa.

Sincerely,

George R. Campbell
Senior Partner

GRC:lpw
Enc. (4)

Introduction

Background of the One Introduced and Relationship to the Writer

Request

8

Letters of Recommendation

Letters of recommendation emphasize how a person worked on a previous job and his expertise. They should also include the relationship between the one seeking the job and the person writing the recommendation.

Introduction

Relationship to the Writer, Background Information, Attributes of the One Recommended

Recommendation

Grant Wood High School
319 30th St. S.E., Cedar Rapids, IA 52403

January 16, 19XX

Linda A. Hagerman, Principal
Thomas Jefferson High School
788 Muscatine Ave.
Iowa City, IA 52240

Dear Ms. Hagerman:

It is with great pleasure that I recommend Mary Alice Westerly for the physics position at Thomas Jefferson.

Mrs. Westerly taught at Grant Wood High School from 1978 to 1986, during which time I was Principal. Her primary teaching responsibilities were physics, chemistry and ninth-grade general science. She was one of the best teachers we have ever had in the area of science, and we were deeply saddened when she and her family moved to Augusta, Maine. I can assure you that if I had a teaching position open in science, I would hire her. She is creative, deeply conscientious, professional and hard-working.

I strongly recommend her and am sure you will be more than satisfied with her performance in the classroom.

Sincerely,

Tom Maxwell, Principal

TJM:mer

Character References

Similar to the letter of recommendation, the character reference refers only to the character of the person. You should include your relationship with the person and how long you have known him.

St. John's-by-the-Lake Episcopal Church
298 Lakeshore Dr., Brandenburg, MN 56315

May 29, 19XX

Klosterman Employment Agency
22 Linden Blvd.
Brandenburg, MN 56315

Dear Sir or Madam:

I have been asked to write a character reference for JoAnn Osterson and am most pleased to do so.

I have known JoAnn since she was three years old when I first moved to Brandenburg. As rector of St. John's-by-the-Lake Episcopal Church, I have been able to watch JoAnn grow and mature into the fine young lady she is today. She is a tireless worker, having given the most volunteer hours of any of our young adults in the parish. She is always cheerful and willingly takes on responsibility.

I am sure that whoever hires her will find her a good worker as well as a pleasant person. She is truly a gem.

Sincerely,

Louis R. Stanley
Rector

LRS:kpw

Introduction

Relationship to the Writer, Background Information, Attributes of the One Recommended

Recommendation

8

Personal Business Letters

Checklist

_____ Is the tone of the letter sincere?

_____ If the letter is a character reference, letter of introduction, or recommendation, did you include how you know the person as a basis of the evaluation?

_____ Did you state the purpose of the letter in the first part?

_____ Did you give background information or details in the second part?

_____ If you used a third part, did you re-congratulate, thank, recommend or set deadlines for your request?

9

Chapter 9 — Letters of Condolence

This chapter includes samples to help you write condolence letters. The broad categories are as follows:

- On the Death of a Business Associate (p. 105)

- On the Death of Mother (p. 106)

- On the Death of Father (p. 107)

- On the Death of Wife (p. 108)

- On the Death of Husband (p. 109)

- On the Death of a Child (p. 110)

- On the Death of a Brother (p. 111)

- On the Death of a Sister (p. 112)

At the side of the page you will find a brief explanation of each part of the letter. The first letter, on page 105, identifies each section of the letter. Subsequent letters identify only changes to the basic format.

Step-by-Step Guide

Although sympathy cards are available, a letter of condolence is more personal. Letters of condolence should be written with a sincere tone. If at all possible, reflect on the person who has died.

Step 1: The first part of the letter offers your condolences.

Step 2: The second part of the letter, if at all possible, should reflect on the person who has died. If you knew the person well, personal recollections are appropriate. If you did not know the person well or at all, this part is optional; although if you can relate his life to your own in some way, you should not skip this part.

Step 3: The last part of the letter offers further condolences or support.

Note: At the end of this chapter is a checklist to use when you write a condolence letter.

Graham's
573 Westdale Rd., Sante Fe, NM 87505

October 6, 19XX

Lou Gosnell, President
Richman's Realty
908 Winky
Sante Fe, NM 87505

Dear Lou:

I was shocked to hear of the death of your partner, Max Wassermann. Although I knew he was ill, I was still taken by surprise by his sudden passing.

Max and I worked together at the old Cramer's Store in downtown Sante Fe when we first arrived here in 1934. I will never forget his immense capacity for helping other people. I share your sorrow at this time.

If there is any way that I can help, please let me know. Rest assured that your loss is all of Sante Fe's loss.

Sincerely,

Geo. "Pinky" Graham

GGG:sok

Date

Inside Address

Salutation

Condolences

Personal Recollection of Deceased

Further Condolences or Offers of Support

Complimentary Close

Signature

Additional Information

9

On the Death of Mother

Condolences

**Personal
Recollection of
Deceased**
(optional)

**Further
Condolences or
Offers of Support**

Trains Unlimited
209 Grant, Quincy, IL 62321

December 11, 19XX

Marilyn Lockwood
542 Maine
Quincy, IL 62322

Dear Marilyn:

Please let me extend my deepest sympathy on behalf of all the staff here at Trains Unlimited on the passing of your mother.

I know that you spoke many times of how difficult your mother's battle with cancer was. I'm sure that, though we are saddened by her death, we share your relief that she is now at peace. She was a brave, courageous woman.

Please accept our sympathy. We have taken up a memorial contribution and sent it to the American Cancer Society in your mother's name.

Sincerely,

Gloria Williams
Vice President, Sales

GAW:vab

Lindlemeier's Tree Farms
R.R. 2, Marlboro, VT 00192

November 1, 19XX

Truk Pham
Box 33
Wyndam, VT 00200

Dear Truk:

I was saddened to hear that your father died last Friday and wish to extend my sympathy.

Although I did not know your father well, I did have a chance to meet him on a couple of occasions. He was proud of his new country and of being able to help his children become established here in the United States. Though his loss is painful, you have much to be proud of with your father.

If there is some way that Tilly and I can help you and your family, let us know. Please take as much time from work as you need to get your father's affairs in order.

Sincerely,

Jake and Tilly Lindlemeier

JEL:mfp

Condolences

Personal Recollection of Deceased (optional)

9

Further Condolences or Offers of Support

On the Death of Wife

Condolences

**Personal
Recollection of
Deceased**
(optional)

**Further
Condolences or
Offers of Support**

Berryhill's Furniture Mart
4455 Southdale Plaza, Portland, OR 97276

March 1, 19XX

Charles M. Potter, Sr.
77 Sunnyset
Portland, OR 97273

Dear Charles:

Please accept our condolences on the untimely passing of
your wife, Lydia. It is difficult to understand why such
tragedies happen, and I do not understand why Lydia was
taken from you so early in your life together.

You must now surround yourself with good friends and the
pleasant memories you have of Lydia. I remember her
beaming smile at the company picnics. She seemed to have
a zest for life that few of us do and was willing to share that
zest with others. I shall never forget her enthusiastic win of
the sack race last year. You would think she had won the
derby as excited as she was.

Please accept what little comfort these words can give you.
If we can help you in any way, please don't hesitate to call.

Sincerely,

N.K. Berryhill

NKB:pmc

Thompson's Janitorial Service
4410 Rodney Dr., Armada, AL 35739

July 17, 19XX

Ida Louise Trotter
555 Keanhorn Split
Jacksontown, AL 36265

Dear Mrs. Trotter:

Our deepest sympathy to you and your family on the death of your husband, Ned. He was a dear friend to so many of us here at Thompson's.

When Ned first came to Thompson's, he told us that he was here to stay and stay he did — 35 years. I am happy that he got to enjoy a few years of his retirement before he became ill. You were fortunate to have so many good years together.

We at Thompson's are here when you need us. Please accept this token as a memorial for Ned.

Sincerely,

George Ray Thompson

GRT:sse

Condolences

Personal Recollection of Deceased

9

Further Condolences or Offers of Support

On the Death of a Child

KFPJ - FM 89.4
212 Kalispell Rd., Butte, MT 59732

February 23, 19XX

Jean and Ike Nelson
R.R. 3
Flying Horn Ranch
Butte, MT 59732

Dear Mr. and Mrs. Nelson:

I was shocked to hear of the death of your son, Bobby. Such
losses defy understanding.

Bobby used to come in on Saturday with Ike to the station
and listen to me do my show. He was forever wanting me to
play John Denver's "Rocky Mountain High." He said it
made him feel good. I'll dedicate it to him this Saturday.

If I can do anything to help, call. Ike, I'll cover for you as
long as you need. God bless.

Sincerely,

Rocky Hopkins

RKH:ilb

Condolences

**Personal
Recollection of
Deceased**
(optional)

**Further
Condolences or
Offers of Support**

On the Death of a Brother

TeleCommunications
239 Tandyview Ct., Arlington, TX 76126

May 12, 19XX

Karen Swanson
7748 Irving Rd. Apt. 354
Arlington, TX 76216

Dear Karen:

I would like to offer my sympathy to you and your family on the passing of your brother.

Although I never met him, I feel as if I know him from all you've said about him at work. I'm sure his wife and children are pleased to know that you spoke so highly of him and his work with mentally retarded children. It is a shame that one so gifted must succumb so early in life.

If you need someone to talk to when you come back, I'll be here.

Sincerely,

Wanda Ferguson
Divisional Manager, TeleMarketing

WAF:bnr

Condolences

Personal Recollection of Deceased
(optional)

Further Condolences or Offers of Support

9

On the Death of a Sister

Condolences

Personal Recollection of Deceased
(optional)

Further Condolences or Offers of Support

Modern Health Insurance Company
909 Blackman Blvd., Hartford, CT 06037

January 4, 19XX

Rita Iverson
2020 Blue Jay
E. Hartford, CT 06087

Dear Rita:

I am most sorry to hear that your sister passed away last week of kidney failure.

Linda Jean was a joy to work with the two years she was here at Modern Health. She always had such outrageous stories to tell. You can be thankful that she enjoyed life while she could.

Please offer my sympathy to your family, especially your mother. I'll take care of your mail while you are gone.

Sincerely,

Terry Glandon
Vice President, Claims

TAG:ccn

Checklist

_____ Is the letter sincere?

_____ Does the first part of the letter offer condolences?

_____ Does the second part of the letter include personal recollections if you knew the deceased?

_____ Does the third part of the letter offer further condolences and support?

_____ Does the letter comfort the bereaved?

9

Chapter 10 — Dealing with Hiring

This chapter has samples of letters you may have to write when hiring new employees. The broad categories are as follows:

- Job Offer (p. 117)

- Rejection of a Solicited Application (p. 118)

- Rejection of an Unsolicited Application (p. 119)

- Reference for Former Employee (p. 120)

- Request for Employment Reference (p. 121)

- Waiver of Confidentiality (p. 122)

At the side of the page you will find a brief explanation of each part of the letter. The first letter, on page 117, identifies each section of the letter. Subsequent letters identify only changes to the basic format.

Step-by-Step Instructions

Letters hiring employees are used by many companies in lieu of a contract drawn up by an attorney and are recognized as legal documents in many courts of law. It is therefore extremely important that you specify each aspect of employment for the prospective employee. Letters in this section also include samples of rejection letters and letters requesting confidential information.

Step 1: The first part of the letter states your purpose. This may be anything from offering a position to requesting information.

Step 2: The second part of the letter gives the details or background information for the first part. If you are offering a position, it is appropriate in this section to give all of the details concerning the position. If you are requesting information, you should explain why you need the information. If you are rejecting an application, you should provide a reason for the rejection.

Step 3: The last part of the letter acts as a summary reminding the recipient of the general nature of the letter.

Note: At the end of this chapter is a checklist to use when you write letters to hire employees.

This letter is used to offer a position to a potential employee and should be treated as a legal contract. It should outline all of the essential information the potential employee needs to make a decision.

Morton Engineering
3457 Randall St. N.E., Armond, AR 72310

January 25, 19XX

J. Wallace Mercer
7898 Talleyho Ln.
Lexington, KY 40329

Dear Mr. Mercer:

It is with great pleasure that I am able to offer you a position at Morton Engineering as an electrical engineer.

The position pays $35,000 annually in equal increments every other Friday. Additionally, you will receive two weeks' paid vacation every 12 months, a bonus equaling two weeks' salary payable the payday before Christmas, health benefits, and $25,000 of life insurance. This position is a two-year agreement after which it may be renegotiated. Either party may terminate with a two-week notice.

We are very pleased to offer you the position and are sure that you will make a superb addition to our firm. If you have any questions, please call me at any time.

Sincerely,

Hanna Westcott
Personnel Director

HJW:kmm

Date

Inside Address

Salutation

Job Offer

Outline the Position

10

Welcome

Complimentary Close

Signature

Additional Information

Rejection of a Solicited Application

This letter is used to inform an applicant that the position for which he applied has been offered to someone else.

	Morton Engineering 3457 Randall St. N.E., Armond, AR 72310 January 25, 19XX K.J. Land 356 Denver University of Nebraska Lincoln, NE 68308 Dear Mr. Land:
Rejection	I am sorry that we are unable to offer you the position of electrical engineer for which you recently interviewed.
Reason for Rejection	We have selected another person who has the type of experience we feel is necessary for the position. I enjoyed interviewing you and hope that you are successful in your employment search in the near future.
Thank You	Thank you for applying at Morton Engineering. If you should have any questions, please call me. Sincerely, Hanna Westcott Personnel Director HJW:kmm

Rejection of an Unsolicited Application

This letter is used to inform an applicant that there are no positions available at the present time for which he is qualified.

First National Bank
223 Ames, Casper, WY 82676

August 30, 19XX

Kelly Flanders
1795 Whisper Ln. #3
Casper, WY 82676

Dear Ms. Flanders:

I am sorry to inform you that we are not presently hiring bank tellers.

As you may know, we recently went through a major expansion. However, we have filled all of our bank teller positions and do not foresee any change in staff in the near future. We will, however, keep your application on file for one year should something arise.

Thank you for your interest in First National. If you should have any questions, please call me.

Sincerely,

Hiram Scott
Vice President Human Resources

HMS:ald

Rejection

Reason for Rejection

10

Thank You

Reference for Former Employee

This letter is a reference for a former employee who is seeking employment elsewhere.

Grant Middle School
901 Third St., Columbia, OH 43230

March 12, 19XX

Wendell R. Rathbourne, Principal
Jasper Heights Middle School
444 Calbryne Rd.
Shaker Heights, OH 44139

Dear Mr. Rathbourne:

Statement of Previous Employment

Pauline O'Malley was employed as a teacher associate at Grant Middle School from April 1988, to June 1988. She was terminated because of a decrease in funding for special education.

Explanation of Performance

During Ms. O'Malley's brief tenure she performed her duties very well. She was a teacher associate for eighth grade behavioral disorders and was well liked by both students and staff. The teachers she worked with speak highly of her ability and willingness to cooperate.

Recommendation

I have no hesitation recommending Ms. O'Malley for any teacher associate position. Please feel free to call me or Marian Thompson, her past supervisor, for further information.

Sincerely,

Lillian M. Detterding
Principal

LMD:gan

Request for Employment Reference

This letter is from a company requesting a reference from a job applicant's previous employer.

TicToc Clocks, Inc.
8071 Speedway, Indianapolis, IN 46107

February 28, 19XX

J. Carson Jamison, President
Weatherman Time
33 Little House Rd.
Columbus, OH 43230

Dear Mr. Jamison:

We recently received an application from Carl Olson for the position of master carpenter with our firm. We understand he was previously employed by you.

We would appreciate any information you could give us concerning Mr. Olson's work habits, expertise as master carpenter, and attitude. We would also appreciate your sharing with us the reason he no longer works for your firm.

We look forward to hearing from you in the near future. Please advise us if the information you provide is confidential. Thank you for your time in answering this request.

Sincerely,

James Vries
President

JBV:llo

Statement of Candidate

Explanation of Request

Thank You

Waiver of Confidentiality

This letter is a form signed by an employee giving the employer permission to provide information to parties such as welfare agencies or spouses who request it. This protects the employer from a lawsuit for invasion of privacy.

Acknowledgment

Permission Given

Wholesome Eggs, Inc.
R.R. 3
Bandville, AL 35542

I, the undersigned, acknowledge that my employer has received a request from Crystal Ziesser for information concerning my employment.

I grant my employer full permission to provide the information described as: salary history, benefit history and sick leave accrued.

Leon Ziesser
_____
Employee

Checklist for Letters Dealing with Hiring

_____ Did you use a positive tone?

_____ Does the letter specify the terms of employment?

_____ Does the letter request specific information?

_____ Did you summarize, thank or restate in the last part of the letter?

_____ If you received the letter, would you know what to do?

Chapter 11 — Customer Relations

This chapter has sample letters that improve or maintain good customer relations. The broad categories are as follows:

At the side of the page, you will find a brief explanation of each part of the letter. The first letter, on page 127, identifies each section of the letter. Subsequent letters identify only changes to the basic format.

Customer Relations Letters

*Recent research sheds
some light on the
importance of
maintaining good
customer relations.
Consider these facts:*

- *96% of unhappy
  customers never let a
  business know they
  are unhappy.*

- *A customer will tell
  an average of 9 to 10
  people about a bad
  experience, but will
  tell only 4 or 5 about
  a good one.*

- *A business will spend
  five times as much to
  acquire a new
  customer as it does
  to service an existing
  one.*

*—adapted from
**Customer Service:
The Key to Winning
Lifetime Customers**
by Marian Thomas;
published by National
Press Publications*

Step-by-Step Guide

These letters are designed to improve or maintain customer relations. The maxim that the customer is always right should be kept in mind while writing these letters. At times, however, you may have to let the customer think he is right while you are proving him wrong!

Step 1: The first part of the letter states your purpose. This may be anything from acknowledging a complaint to announcing new products.

Step 2: The second part of the letter explains the purpose. If the first part acknowledges a complaint, then the second part explains what you are going to do about it. If the first part announces new products to valued customers, then the second part gives the details about those products.

Step 3: The last part is the sugar to leave a good taste in the customer's mouth. It summarizes the letter, thanks the customer and reiterates the customer's value to your organization.

Note: At the end of this chapter is a checklist to use when you write a customer relations letter.

General Appreciation

This letter is used to show appreciation for your customers. It may be used as a sales and promotion letter or a thank-you for continued patronage.

Zebra Prints **224 Bever Ave., Madrid, MS 39378**	
October 12, 19XX	**Date**
Lillian R. Wilkinson 4500 Ramble Road Lane Madrid, MS 39379	**Inside Address**
Dear Ms. Wilkinson:	**Salutation**
On behalf of Zebra Prints we wish to express our sincerest appreciation for your continued patronage. It is because of valued customers like you that we are able to continue to offer you the finest in fabrics.	**Statement of Purpose**
As you probably know, Zebra Prints has been in business for 75 years. We are dedicated to bringing you the finest in fabrics, particularly those of all-natural materials. Mr. Case, our founding father, loved to say, "The customer wants the best at the lowest price," and that is the motto we use as our guiding principle.	**Elaboration**
Please stop in and see us soon. Our new spring fabrics will be in the showroom on March 15. If you bring this letter with you, we will give you a 15% discount on any fabric you purchase in March.	**Summary and Appreciation**
Sincerely yours,	**Complimentary Close**
Terrance Sullivan Case, Jr. President	**Signature**
TSC:maj	**Additional Information**

11

127

Acknowledging a Complaint

This letter is used to acknowledge a complaint and offer a solution to the problem.

Tiny Toes Dance Studio
33 Barbara Drive, Butte, MT 59777

September 2, 19XX

Mickey Wu
790 7th St.
Butte, MT 59777

Dear Mr. Wu:

Acknowledgment of Complaint

Thank you for your letter of August 30 discussing our policy concerning payment of missed classes.

Solution

I have checked with our owner, Ms. Timberlane, for a clarification. In the past our policy was that missed classes would still need to be paid for. Under the circumstances, however, she said that you will not have to pay for the classes your daughter missed because of her unfortunate accident on the way to class.

Summary and Thank You

We hope this is a satisfactory solution for you and wish your daughter, Jasmine, a speedy recovery. We shall put a hold on your account until she is ready to return to her tap lessons. Thank you once again for your concern and understanding.

Sincerely yours,

Mary Manson
Business Manager

MLM:wmj

Regaining a Customer's Confidence

This letter is used to smooth relations with a disgruntled customer and regain his confidence in your firm.

Modern Medical Supplies
302 Main, Portland, OR 97272

November 23, 19XX

Dr. Laura Schmitt
1520 Barston Blvd.
Sacramento, CA 95808

Dear Dr. Schmitt:

Please accept our sincerest apologies on the recent mixup concerning the shipment of tongue depressors. I can assure you that action has been taken to remedy the problem in our warehouse.

As a token of good faith we have deducted 15% from your bill. We hope that this will help compensate for any inconvenience this problem caused. We have dismissed our head shipping clerk because of this unfortunate incident. After checking, we discovered a number of glaring errors he had made. Thank you for bringing the error to our attention.

We hope that this will be a satisfactory solution. Your corrected order of tongue depressors should be arrive shortly as they were sent November 22.

Sincerely yours,

Graham Johnson
Customer Relations

GJJ:amr

Statement of Purpose

Regaining of Confidence

Summary and Thank You

11

129

Customer Relations Letters

Acknowledging a Complaint — Disclaiming Responsibility

This letter acknowledges a customer's complaint in order to maintain good relations; however, it refers the customer to another source that is responsible for the problem.

Peoria Pet Foods
3005 Lincolnway, Peoria, IL 61635

March 30, 19XX

Mary Louise Jones
Paws R Us
8900 Waconia, Joliet, IL 60434

Dear Ms. Jones:

Acknowledgment of Complaint

Thank you for bringing the problem of late deliveries to our attention. I'm sure they must be most aggravating.

Disclaimer of Responsibility

As much as we would like to help you, the problem lies with the trucking firm and not here at Peoria Pet Foods. We have contacted them concerning the late deliveries and are reviewing our use of Nelson Trucking as our carrier. At present we have no contract with them, but shall be demanding a contract so that we have leverage in such matters. I suggest that you contact them also as they seem unconcerned about the situation.

Apology and Thank You

I'm sorry I can't help you any more than this, but I can assure you that we are trying to remedy the situation as quickly as we can. Unfortunately, an immediate solution is dependent upon Nelson Trucking. Thank you once again for your understanding.

Sincerely yours,

Lucy McAlister
Customer Relations

LJM:glu

Acknowledging a Complaint — Explaining a Misunderstanding

This letter acknowledges a customer's complaint in order to maintain good relations by explaining a misunderstanding between the customer and the business.

RTM, Inc.
P.O. Box 2089, Milwaukee, WI 53219

January 16, 1990

Thomas R. Linder
Bottlers' Distributors
7035 Wacker
Milwaukee, WI 53227

Dear Mr. Linder:

I appreciate your bringing to my attention the problem of our Colden Beer and its introductory flyer. I understand your confusion perfectly.

When we sent you the letter introducing our new beer our marketing department mistakenly sent a mock-up of an ad for Eagle's Wings Ale. Naturally, you would be confused because we were referring to the blue eagle on Colden Beer while giving you the bald eagle label of Eagle's Wings Ale. We are most sorry for this error and have enclosed a corrected flyer. Needless to say, our marketing department is red-faced.

I'm sorry that this unfortunate misunderstanding came about and hope that this letter and the enclosed corrected flyer clears up this matter. Thank you once again for bringing this to my attention.

Sincerely,

R. Edward Randsford
Public Relations Director

RER:kks

Acknowledgment of Complaint

Explaining the Misunderstanding

11

Apology and Thank You

Correcting an Error

This letter is used to correct an error that either the customer caught or that the business caught.

Statement of Error

Correction of Error

Apology and Thank You

Capital Credit Union
890 Minnesota Ave, Washington, D.C. 20041

April 24, 19XX

Mr. and Mrs. John Gallup
3256 Mozart Dr.
Silver Springs, MD 20743

Dear Mr. and Mrs. Gallup:

After our current auditing we discovered an underpayment to your account of $53.23 in interest.

The error occurred in the transferring of funds in March from your High-Fi account to your regular savings account. We have corrected your savings account and credited you with $53.23.

I hope this is satisfactory, and I apologize for any confusion this error caused. Thank you for your continued patronage.

Sincerely,

Molly Butters
Vice-President, Accounting

MMB:tli

General Apology

This letter is used to apologize to customers.

Merkers Department Store
1115 Brandon, New Ulm, MN 56053

July 22, 19XX

Kim Langworth
R.R.1
Red Earth, MN 56670

Dear Ms. Langworth:

We at Merker's would like to extend our sincerest apologies and ask for your understanding.

Our recent sales brochure made claims that we could not follow through on. We led you to believe that all merchandise in the Summer Saver Sale was on sale for 50% off. The printer inadvertently left out the important word "selected." Because of this glaring error, we have decided to postpone our sale and reschedule it for another time. By postponing the sale we will be able to offer you even better bargains than we had originally planned.

Thank you for your understanding in this embarrassing situation.

Sincerely,

R. Merker
Chairman of the Board

RCM:hhh

Apology

Explanation

Apology and Thank You

11

Acknowledging an Order — Back Order

This letter is used to acknowledge that a customer's order has been received, but that it is back-ordered, thus causing a delay.

Acknowledgment of Order

Explanation and Offer of an Alternative (optional)

Apology and Thank You

Todmann Nuts and Bolts
P.O. Box 3445, Idaho Falls, ID 83406

June 3, 19XX

Timothy R. Johnson, Purchasing
Sheppard Hardware Distributors
P.O. Box 1078
Kansas City, MO 64109-1078

Dear Mr. Johnson:

We are pleased to receive your order for 10,000 quarter-inch nuts, part number XK22345JM. However, we are unable at this time to fulfill that order.

Our present inventory has been depleted and that nut is now on back-order until mid-July. Our supplier of raw materials is unable to supply the materials until July 1, thus pushing us back to mid-July for possible delivery. We have tried, but were unsuccessful, to find an alternate source of raw materials. If you like, we could substitute part number XK22346JM. It is a penny higher in price per unit. Otherwise, we will keep your order and rush it to you as soon as we can start production on these nuts again.

Thank you for your understanding in this matter. We apologize for your inconvenience.

Sincerely,

Cass Walker
Production Head

CBW:pst

Acknowledging an Order — Explaining Shipment Procedures

This letter is used to explain a shipping procedure to a customer while acknowledging that an order has been received.

Raging Bull Farms
R.R.2, Kingman, OK 73439

August 13, 19XX

Natalie Gorman
Cherokee Crafts
900 E. Main
Tulsa, OK 74102

Dear Ms. Gorman:

Thank you for your order of 25 authentic Cherokee head-dresses on August 11, 19XX. We will be sending those immediately.

Because of the fragile nature of our head-dresses, we hand deliver to our customers within Oklahoma. Our delivery day for Tulsa is Friday which means that your head-dresses will arrive this coming Friday, August 17. If this is unsatisfactory, please call us so that we can arrange an alternative delivery date.

Thank you for your business. I'm sure that you will be most pleased with our head-dresses, and we look forward to working with you in the future.

Sincerely yours,

Tamara Whitewater

TJW:zmd

Acknowledgment of Order

Explanation

Thank You

11

135

Apologizing for an Employee's Action

This letter is used to apologize for the action of one of your employees who has damaged customer relations.

Belle's Phone Store
Windale Mall
8855 Outer Drive, Waukegan, IL 60079

November 3, 19XX

Travis C. Schultz
5554 Rocky Shore Dr.
North Waukegan, IL 60079

Dear Mr. Schultz:

Apology

I wish to personally apologize for your unfortunate treatment by our employee, Betty Robertson, last Friday. Her actions toward you were totally inappropriate.

Action Taken
(optional)

Because of this situation, we have relieved Ms. Robertson of her position. We would also like to offer you a gift certificate for $50 of merchandise at our store. We value our customers and hope that this token will help compensate for the embarrassment you felt. We are increasing our training in customer relations for all of our employees to avoid just such a problem occurring again.

Thank You

Thank you for your business and your understanding. We hope that this is a satisfactory solution to the problem.

Sincerely yours,

Belle June Maples

BJM:kio

Announcing New Products to Select Group of Customers

This letter is used to announce new products to a select group of regular customers. It may be seen as a sales pitch.

Ft. Dodge Appliances
563 Grand Ave., Ft. Dodge, IA 50569

October 30, 19XX

Caroline M. Ness
R.R. 3
Gowrie, IA 50337

Dear Ms. Ness:

Ft. Dodge Appliances is pleased to announce our new line of Wonder Work Appliances. We are now the authorized Wonder Work dealer for Ft. Dodge.

Wonder Work Appliances, established for three decades in the East, is now expanding to the Midwest, and we are excited to be part of their expanding network. They specialize in small appliances that are known throughout the industry for their quality and durability. So you have a chance to see them at work, we have arranged to demonstrate them this Saturday, November 3, at our store from 9 to 5. Special discounts are available if you bring this letter with you.

Thank you for your continued business. We look forward to seeing you this Saturday.

Sincerely,

Barney Carlson

BAC:eeo

Announcement

Elaboration

Thank You

11

Announcing a Sales Campaign to Preferred Customers

This letter is used to announce a sales campaign to preferred customers, thus giving them a head start in purchasing, or offering them further reduced prices.

Announcement

Elaboration

Thank You

Green Mountain Antiques Wholesale
Stapleton, VT 05020

January 19, 19XX

Max Castle
Heavenly Daze Antiques
Wiloughby, NH 03308

Dear Mr. Castle:

Green Mountain Antiques Wholesale will be holding our Winter Sale from February 12-16.

As a preferred customer, you are invited to attend a pre-sale showing on February 11 with discounts up to 50% on specially marked items. We feel that this is just one small way that we can repay you for all of your business over the years. Our enclosed flyer shows you some of the outstanding values available.

Thank you for your business. I hope we will see you on February 11.

Sincerely,

Madeline O'Shea

MAO:ser

Enc.

Announcing a Price Increase

This letter is used to announce a price increase and soften the blow to the customer.

Grand Greetings, Inc.
330 Big Bend St., Charleston, SC 29410

February 22, 19XX

Harry C. Marker
Card Distributors, Ltd.
11 Fillmore
Atlanta, GA 30325

Dear Mr. Marker:

Grand Greetings, Inc. is announcing a price increase in our Wacky Writers Line. Because of increased production costs it is necessary to increase prices by 10%.

In order to continue to produce a high-quality product, we have recently installed new high-speed, high-definition printing presses. This, along with the increased price of paper, has forced us to increase our prices. I have enclosed a brochure with the new prices in it for your benefit.

Thank you for your understanding in this matter. We feel that these increases will still allow you to sell these cards at competitive prices.

Sincerely,

K. Charles Grand
President

KCG:lpw
Enc.

Announcement

Elaboration

Thank You

11

Customer Relations Letters

Notifying Customers of a Move

This letter is used to notify customers of a move and to assure them that the move will not affect them or will be advantageous to them.

Announcement

Elaboration

Summary

Marco Paper Clips
P.O. Box 22, Marquette, MI 49855

May 4, 19XX

K.J Wasserman
City Business Supply
763 C. St. S.W.
Columbia, MO 65205

Dear Mr. Wasserman:

On July 1, 19XX, Marco Paper Clips will be moving to Des Moines, Iowa. This move should greatly benefit your company.

We are excited about the move to Des Moines. Our move will help you receive shipments more quickly. It will also reduce the cost of shipping to Marco and we can pass those savings on to you. Des Moines' larger labor market also allows us to expand our facilities and product line. We feel that this will definitely benefit our customers.

Please feel free to contact us if you have any concerns. Our new address in Des Moines will be: Marco Paper Clips, 3567 Grandview, Des Moines, IA 54421. Our toll-free number will be 800-BUY-CLIP.

Sincerely,

G. Antonio Marco
President

GAM:etv
Enc.

Holiday Greetings

This letter is used to send holiday greetings to your customers.

Flatt Tire Co.
223 Nueva Matica, Santa Cruz, CA 95066

December 5, 19XX

Theodore "Bubba" Brown
Glendale Amoco
Highway 13
Glendale, CA 90046

Dear Mr. Brown:

Flatt Tire Co. would like to wish you and your employees the very best this holiday season. We hope that you are blessed with customers as nice as you.

We are most fortunate to have customers like Glendale Amoco and hope that this coming new year we can continue our relationship. We know that our prosperity depends on the efforts of our customers.

Thank you for helping make Flatt Tire Co. one of the leaders in Southern California. Our fondest regards for all of you at Glendale Amoco.

Happy Holidays,

Rhonda J. Flatt
President

RJF:alc

Greetings

Elaboration
(optional)

Thank You

11

Customer Relations Letters

Checklist

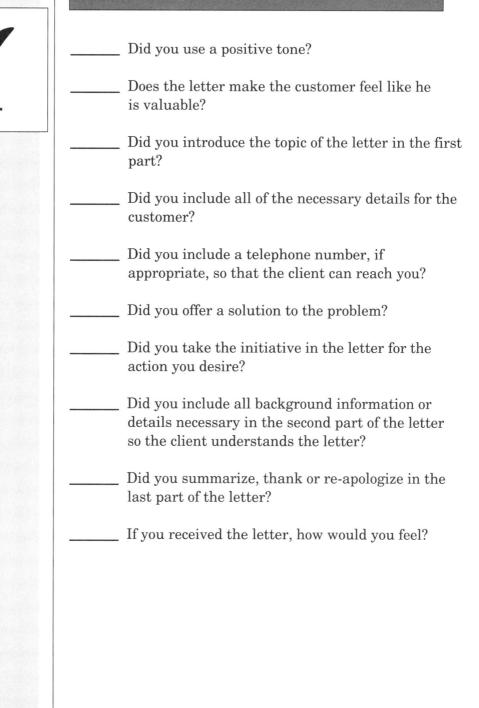

_____ Did you use a positive tone?

_____ Does the letter make the customer feel like he is valuable?

_____ Did you introduce the topic of the letter in the first part?

_____ Did you include all of the necessary details for the customer?

_____ Did you include a telephone number, if appropriate, so that the client can reach you?

_____ Did you offer a solution to the problem?

_____ Did you take the initiative in the letter for the action you desire?

_____ Did you include all background information or details necessary in the second part of the letter so the client understands the letter?

_____ Did you summarize, thank or re-apologize in the last part of the letter?

_____ If you received the letter, how would you feel?

12

Chapter 12 — Media Letters

This chapter has samples to help you write letters to the media (newspapers, television stations, magazines, etc.). The broad categories are as follows:

At the side of the page, you will find a brief explanation of each part of the letter. The first letter, on page 145, identifies each section of the letter. Subsequent letters identify only changes to the basic format.

Media Letters

Media letters are used in business as a way to get the public's attention. Media exposure is free advertising and the smart business person uses it to sell his business and its services or products. The letter in and of itself is a sales tool.

Step 1: The first part of the letter or press release states your purpose. This may be anything from announcing a new employee to responding to an editorial.

Step 2: The second part of the letter or press release explains the first part by giving details and examples about the first part. This part should include all pertinent information concerning the event or situation. If, for example, you are announcing a new employee, you would in the second part give the details about the employee. Always answer the questions Who? What? When? Where? Why? and if appropriate, How much? in this section.

Step 3: The last part of the letter acts as a summary reminding the recipient of the general nature of the letter. It may also be used as a thank-you.

Note: At the end of this chapter is a checklist to use when you write a media letter.

Media Event Letter — Sales Campaign Kickoff

This letter is used to alert the media to a sales campaign kickoff and invite the media to cover the event.

Capital Crystal
449 Worthington, Charleston WV 25009

March 16, 19XX

Todd Phillips, Station Manager
KOAL
2525 Kanawah
Charleston, WV 25009

Dear Mr. Phillips:

On March 25, Capital Crystal will announce the winner of our "How Many Goblets in a Dump Truck" contest. We will do so at noon in front of our business at 449 Worthington.

Our "How Many Goblets in a Dump Truck" contest has been going on now for approximately three months and someone will be the lucky winner of $1,000. We will also donate $1,000 to Charleston's Homeless Shelter at that time. With the announcement we will dump the goblets out of the truck and onto the ground. Wade Wilson and His Debonnaires will play during the reception that follows.

We are sure that this event would be of interest to viewers of "Eye on Charleston" at noon because of the huge response we have had to the contest. Thank you for your interest.

Sincerely yours,

Candice Trotter
President

CJT:lsj

Date

Inside Address

Salutation

Announcement

Explanation

Summary and Thank You

Complimentary Close

Signature

Additional Information

12

Media Event Letter — Recently Published Book

This letter is used to alert the media to a recently published book.

Donaldson's
223 Niagara Dr., Buffalo, NY 14290

September 12, 19XX

Mary Beth Parkinson
WWJ
874 7th St.
Buffalo, NY 14292

Dear Ms. Parkinson:

Announcement

I have recently published a book called *Entrepreneur at Risk*. I am sending you a copy to review.

Explanation

I think the topic is worthy of your morning show, "Good Morning Buffalo," and I would be interested in discussing the book as a guest on your show. The premise is that entrepreneurs are at risk in the U.S. and will soon be an endangered species. This is a very timely topic with an upcoming forum on entrepreneurs at the Carmine Colosseum.

Summary and Thank You

I have enclosed my biographical sketch, a synopsis of the book, and a press release from my publishing house. I hope that you will have time to look at these. Thank you for your interest.

Sincerely,

Larry J. Beiers
President

LJB:wuy

This letter is used to alert the media of a company's anniversary.

Evanson Buick
7793 Sahara Way, Reno, NV 89585

May 19, 19XX

Wayne Wilson
KBET
444 Plaza Dr.
Reno, NV 89588

Dear Mr. Wilson:

On May 29 Evanson Buick will be 50 years old, making us the oldest car dealership in Nevada. We will be staging a three-day celebration.

On May 29, we will kickoff our anniversary with free hot air balloon rides and an ascension at 6 p.m. On May 30, we will have the oldest race car driver, Judd MacElroy, signing autographs from 2 to 4 p.m. On May 31, we will have our drawing for a Buick Reatta at 5:30 p.m. followed by a picnic open to the public. During all three days there will be displays of antique autos and carnival rides for the children. We think that our anniversary event would make a fine spot on your "Neighbors" segment on the six o'clock news.

I have enclosed a flyer describing the complete festivities. Thank you for helping us celebrate our anniversary.

Sincerely,

M. Art Evanson
President

MAE:fsw
Enc.

Announcement

Explanation

Summary and Thank You

12

147

Press Release — Anniversary

This press release is used to alert the media of a company's anniversary.

Announcement

Explanation

Darling's Cookies
309 Watertown Rd., Tacoma, WA 98438

January 29, 19XX
FOR IMMEDIATE RELEASE

On February 5, 19XX, Darling's Cookies will celebrate its 50th anniversary, making us the oldest bakery in Tacoma and the second oldest in the Tri-State area.

Darling's Cookies was established on February 5, 1940, by Darrel Darling. At first, Darling's only employed three people and was located on Front St. in downtown Tacoma. After the war, Darling's moved to its present location on Watertown Rd. and now employs 25 full-time people. Darling's specialties are cinnamon rolls, chocolate chip cookies, and its patented double chocolate fudge bar. Darling's will host an open house on February 5 at its plant.

FOR MORE INFORMATION CONTACT:
Darrel Darling, Jr.
President

Press Release — Speaking Engagement

This press release is used to alert the media of an upcoming speech.

Los Gatos Community College
2312 College Dr. Los Gates, NM 87531

April 2, 19XX
FOR IMMEDIATE RELEASE

Dr. Larry Thompson, noted historian, will speak April 20, 1990, at Los Gatos Community College. He will speak on "History in the Making: How Current Events Redefine Our Lives."

Dr. Thompson is a leading authority on trends in history. He is professor of History from Cornell University in Ithaca, NY. He is presently on leave from the university so that he can lecture around the world on this topic. His speech has been well-received throughout the United States. He will explain how the recent fall of the Berlin Wall has affected all of us even though we have not yet identified that it has. After the speech Dr. Thompson will hold a symposium on American business trends. He will autograph copies of his best seller, *Wake Up America*, in the lobby of the Emerson Auditorium prior to his speech at 7 p.m.

FOR MORE INFORMATION CONTACT: Sara Thompson, Public Relations Dept., Los Gates Community College

Announcement

Explanation

12

149

Press Release — Promotion

This press release is used to alert the media of a promotion within your business.

Announcement

Explanation

Ogden Manufacturing
58 Brigham Young Dr., Ogden, UT 84404

August 30, 19XX
FOR IMMEDIATE RELEASE

Ogden Manufacturing announces the promotion of Paul K. Van Daan to Vice President, Accounting. He will replace Terrance Reilly who is retiring.

Paul Van Daan joined Ogden Manufacturing in March 19XX, as an accountant and was promoted in 19XX to Department Head, Accounts Receivable. In 19XX he was promoted to Division Head, Customer Relations. He is a graduate of Brigham Young University and is a Certified Public Accountant. Previously, he worked for Dowling Box, Ltd.

FOR MORE INFORMATION CONTACT: David Conrad, Human Resources Office, Ogden Manufacturing

A black and white photo is enclosed.

Press Release — New Employee

This press release is used to announce to the media that a new employee will be joining your firm.

Klinger Blinds
2221 Washington, Flagstaff, AZ 86093

October 17, 19XX
FOR IMMEDIATE RELEASE

Klinger Blinds announces that Karen M. Bark has been hired as our Director of Sales. She will start in her new position on November 1.

Karen M. Bark is a native of Southern California and has previously been employed by Tremore Window Treatments in Los Angeles as Sales Coordinator. She has her degree in Interior Design from the Design Institute in San Francisco. Ms. Bark's design for the Home Lovely's "Home Beautification Project" won her first place last year in the prestigious competition.

FOR MORE INFORMATION CONTACT: Trish Klinger, Klinger Blinds

A black and white photo is enclosed.

Announcement

Explanation

12

Response to Editorial — Positive

This letter is used to respond to an editorial when your firm is in agreement.

Announcement

Explanation

Thank You

Greater Augusta Merchants
651 Main, Augusta, ME 04326

September 22, 19XX

Bonnie Ervin, Station Director
WKLT Radio
1500 Walker
Augusta, ME 04325

Dear Ms. Ervin:

We, the Greater Augusta Merchants, wish to commend you for the stand you have taken against parking meters in downtown Augusta. Your editorial of September 20 was well thought out.

We feel that placing parking meters in downtown Augusta will discourage our customers from coming downtown to shop. Your report of other nearby cities who have recently installed parking meters and have seen a drop in customers demonstrates that we could create the same problem if the city government passes this ordinance. We strongly urge you to continue to speak out against this issue.

Thank you for your support for our position.

Sincerely,

Marvin Quackenbush
Executive Secretary

MJQ:omr

Response to Editorial — Negative

This letter is used to respond to an editorial when your firm is in disagreement.

Greater Augusta Merchants
651 Main, Augusta, ME 04326

October 20, 19XX

Bonnie Ervin, Station Director
WKLT Radio
1500 Walker
Augusta, ME 04326

Dear Ms. Ervin:

Although we agree with your previous editorials opposing parking meters in downtown Augusta, we are not in agreement with your editorial of last night. We can see no value in turning the downtown business district into a mall-like area.

To resurface our streets and make them into malls will irreversibly damage businesses downtown. The city engineers estimate the mall project will disrupt business for a minimum of a full year. Many downtown businesses are now struggling to stay alive and the mall project would be their death knell. Additionally, when completed, we would have 50% fewer parking places for our customers. Perhaps the downtown area does need cosmetic surgery, but not when it devastates the economy of downtown.

Thank you for your understanding of our opposition. We hope that you will reconsider your position.

Sincerely,

Marvin Quackenbush
Executive Secretary

MJQ:omr

Announcement

Explanation

Thank You

12

Asking to Make a Speech

This is a letter that is used when you want to make a speech or presentation.

J. P. Gaslight and Co.
790 Eastern Ave., Ithaca, NY 14743

May 7, 19XX

Calvin S. Snyder, Program Chairman
Environmental Institute
445 J. Ave. East
Lincoln, NE 68302

Dear Mr. Snyder:

Request

I would like to be put on the program of the upcoming Environmental Institute Workshop in October 1990, in Chicago. I feel that my presentation on acid rain and its effect on the northeastern United States fits in with your theme, "Environmental Consequences."

Explanation

I have enclosed an outline of my proposed presentation. As you can see, my recent research for our firm shows the irreversible damage done to the northeastern United States by acid rain. The presentation I have outlined has been well-received at the Global Earth Conference in Boston and last week at the Toronto Conference for Environmental Concerns. I have also enclosed a list of other presentations I have given on environmental issues.

Thank You

Thank you for your prompt consideration.

Sincerely,

Ted Whiteman

TKW:cap
Enc.

Asking for a Correction

This is a letter used to request that a correction be made from a published or televised report.

Williams and Sons
1002 Elm St., Topeka, KS 66404

August 11, 19XX

Arthur Church, Managing Editor
Topeka Times
333 Main
Topeka, KS 66402

Dear Mr. Church:

Your article about Williams and Sons in last Sunday's *Times* was most appreciated. However, there is one small correction that needs to be made.

In the article you stated that Williams and Sons has grown 15% in the last year. In reality we have grown 25% in the last year, 15% of that being in the last month. Perhaps this seems like a trivial matter, but the smaller number is negative publicity for Williams. Would you please make a correction in your upcoming business news section this Sunday?

Thank you for your prompt consideration. We appreciate the fine job you have been doing.

Sincerely,

C. Blake Williams
President

CBW:nbc

Correction

Explanation

Thank You

12

Media Letters

Checklist

_____ Did you use a positive tone?

_____ Does the letter sell itself?

_____ Did you introduce the topic of the letter in the first part?

_____ Did you include all of the necessary details for the media such as date, time and place of event?

_____ Did you include a name so that you can be reached for verification?

_____ Did you include all background information or details necessary in the second part of the letter?

_____ Did you summarize or thank in the last part of the letter?

_____ If you received the letter, would you do what you are asking the recipient to do?

Index

Index

I

I

Index

I

Index

I

A

Appendix — Forms of Address

Addressee
> Form of Address
>> Salutation

Clerical and Religious Orders

Abbot
> The Right Reverend Walter Jones, O.S.B.
> Right Reverend and Abbot of St. Benedicts
> Dear Father:

Archbishop
> The Most Reverend Archbishop of Canada
>> Your Excellency: or
>> Dear Archbishop
> The Most Reverend Archbishop Terrance Smith:
> Archbishop of Canada

Archbishop, Anglican
> To His Grace the Lord Archbishop of Canterbury
>> Your Grace:
>> My Dear Archbishop:

Archdeacon
> The Venerable the Archdeacon of New York
>> Venerable Sir:

Bishop, Catholic
The Most Reverend Andrew Duncan
Your Excellency:
Bishop of New York
Dear Bishop Duncan:

Bishop, Episcopal
The Right Reverend Samuel Thomas
Right Reverend Sir:
Bishop of South Carolina
Dear Bishop Thomas:

Bishop, Other Denominations
The Reverend Sandra Wright
Reverend Madam:
Dear Bishop Wright:

Brotherhood, Catholic, Member of
Brother Williams, S.J.
Dear Brother James:

Brotherhood, Catholic, Superior of
Brother Edward, S.J., Superior
Dear Brother Edward:

Canon
The Reverend Dwight Boyd
Dear Canon Boyd:

Cardinal
His Eminence
Your Eminence:
Harold Cardinal Lyte
Dear Cardinal Lyte:

Clergyman, Protestant

The Reverend Catherine Wilson
    Dear Madam:
    Dear Ms. Wilson:
        (or, if having a doctor's degree)
The Reverend Dr. John Wong
    Dear Dr. Wong:

Dean (of a Cathedral)

The Very Reverend Calvin Schmidt
    Very Reverend Sir:
Dean Calvin Schmidt
    Dear Dean Schmidt:

Monsignor

The Right Reverend Monsignor Ellis
    Dear Monsignor Ellis:

Patriarch (of an Eastern Church)

His Beatitude the Patriarch of New York
    Most Reverend Lord:

Pope

His Holiness Pope John
    Your Holiness:
His Holiness the Pope
    Most Holy Father:

Priest

The Reverend Father Martin
    Dear Father Martin:
The Reverend Lynn Martin
    Dear Father:

Priest, Episcopal

The Reverend Edward Arnold
    Dear Mr. Arnold:
    Dear Father Arnold:

A

Rabbi
> Rabbi Eli Gossman
>> Dear Rabbi Gossman:
>>> (if having a doctor's degree)
>> Rabbi David Weiss, D.D.
>>> Dear Dr. Weiss:

Sisterhood, member of
> Sister Mary Theresa, S. C.
>> Dear Sister Mary Theresa:
>> Dear Sister:

Sisterhood, Superior of
> The Reverend Mother Superior, S.C.
> Reverend Mother:

College and University Officials

Dean of a College or University
> Dean Mary Carlson
>> Dear Dean Carlson:

President of a College or University
> President James Bagg
>> Dear President Bagg:

Professor at a College or University
> Professor Linda Tripp
>> Dear Professor Tripp:

Note: The college official's degrees, if known, may be added after the name.

Diplomats

Ambassador to the U.S.
His Excellency Reginald Butters
Ambassador of Bermuda
Sir:
Dear Mr. Ambassador:

American Ambassador
The Honorable J. Ellen Standford
American Ambassador
Madam:
Dear Ms. Ambassador:

American Charge d'Affaires
Allen White, Esq.
American Charge d'Affaires
Dear Sir:

Minister to the U.S.
The Honorable Harry Lindermann
Minister of Liechtenstein
Sir:
Dear Mr. Minister:

Secretery-General, U.N.
Her Excellency Nbutu Montabi
Secretary-General of the United Nations
Excellency:
Dear Ms. Secretary-General:

A

Appendix — Forms of Address

Federal, State, and Local Government Officials

Alderman
The Honorable Harriett Monson
Dear Ms. Monson:

Assemblyman
See Representative, State

Associate Justice, Supreme Court
Mr. Arthur Riley
The Supreme Court of the United States
Dear Mr. Justice:

Cabinet Officers:

Secretary of State
Secretary of State
The Honorable Emily Williamson
Dear Madam:

The Attorney General
The Honorable Martin Trymore
Attorney General of the United States
Dear Sir:

Chief Justice, Supreme
The Chief Justice of the United States
Dear Mr. Chief :

Court
Justice:

Commissioner
The Honorable C. Thomas Black
Dear Mr. Black:

Former U.S. President
    The Honorable Wilson Edwards
        Dear Mr. Edwards:

Governor
    The Honorable Mary Simpson
    Governor of Utah
        Dear Governor Simpson:

Judge, Federal
    The Honorable Tomas Gonzales
    United States District Judge
        Dear Judge Gonzales:

Judge, State or Local
    Chief Judge of the Court of Appeals
    The Honorable Larry Nelson
        Dear Judge Nelson:

Lieutenant Governor
    The Honorable Aaron Gudenkauf
    Lieutenant Governor of New Jersey
        Dear Mr. Gudenkauf:

Mayor
    The Honorable W. M. Tied
    Mayor of Greenville
        Dear Mayor Tied:

President, U.S.
    The President
        Dear Mr. President:

Representative, State (Same format for assemblyman)
    The Honorable Amanda Brown
        Dear Ms. Brown:
        House of Representatives
        State Capitol

A

Appendix — Forms of Address

Representative, U.S.
The United States House of Representatives
The Honorable Blake Grahame
Dear Mr. Grahame:

Senator, State
The Honorable Matthew K. Billings
Dear Senator Billings:
The State Senate
State Capitol

Senator, U.S.
The Honorable Lillian Vries
Dear Senator Vries:
United States Senate

Speaker, U.S. House
The Honorable James B. Castle
Dear Mr. Speaker:

Representatives
Speaker of the House of Representatives

Vice-President, U.S.
The Vice-President
Dear Mr. Vice-President:
United States Senate

Military Ranks

Admiral, Vice-Admiral, Rear Admiral
(Full Rank + Full Name + Comma + Abbreviation of Branch of Service)
Sir:
Dear Admiral Rhodes:

Airman

(Full Rank + Full Name + Comma + Abbreviation of Branch of Service)
Dear Airman Smith:

Cadet

Cadet Jack Roberts
United States Military Academy
Dear Cadet Roberts:

Captain (Air Force, Army, Coast Guard, Marine Corps, or Navy)

(Full Rank + Full Name + Comma + Abbreviation of Branch of Service)
Dear Captain Lane:

Colonel, Lieutenant Colonel (Air Force, Army, or Marine Corps)

(Full Rank + Full Name + Comma + Abbreviation of Branch of Service)
Dear Captain Arnold:

Commander (Coast Guard or Navy)

(Full Rank + Full Name + Comma + Abbreviation of Branch of Service)
Dear Commander Grove:

Corporal

(Full Rank + Full Name + Comma + Abbreviation of Branch of Service)
Dear Corporal Jones:

First Lieutenant, Second Lieutenant (Air Force, Army, or Marine Corps)

(Full Rank + Full Name + Comma + Abbreviation of Branch of Service)
Dear Lieutenant O'Shannon:

A

General, Lieutenant General, Major General, Brigadier General (Air Force, Army, or Marine Corps)

(Full Rank + Full Name + Comma + Abbreviation of Branch of Service)

Sir:

Dear General Tubbs:

Lieutenant Commander, Lieutenant, Lieutenant (JG), Ensign (Coast Guard, Navy)

(Full Rank + Full Name + Comma + Abbreviation of Branch of Service)

Dear Mr. Crites:

Major (Air Force, Army, or Marine Corps)

(Full Rank + Full Name + Comma + Abbreviation of Branch of Service)

Dear Major Giles:

Master Sergeant (an example of other enlisted ranks having compound titles not shown here)

(Full Rank + Full Name + Comma + Abbreviation of Branch of Service)

Dear Sergeant Kaye:

Midshipman

Midshipman Sally Cole

United States Naval Academy

Dear Midshipman Cole:

Petty Officer and Chief Petty Officer Ranks

(Full Rank + Full Name + Comma + Abbreviation of Branch of Service)

Dear Mr. Schmidt:

Dear Mr. Trank: or

Dear Chief Trank:

Private

(Full Rank + Full Name + Comma + Abbreviation of Branch of Service)

Dear Private Hesse:

Seaman

(Full Rank + Full Name + Comma + Abbreviation of Branch of Service)

> Dear Seaman Waters:

Specialist

(Full Rank + Full Name + Comma + Abbreviation of Branch of Service)

> Dear Mr. Ledford:

Other Ranks Not Listed

(Full Rank + Full Name + Comma + Abbreviation of Branch of Service)

Military Abbreviations

Army	U.S.A.
Air Force	U.S.A.F.
Marine	U.S.M.C.
Navy	U.S.N.

Professional Ranks and Titles

Attorney

Mr. R. Allan Whiteman Attorney-at-Law
or R. Allan Whiteman, Esq.

> Dear Mr. Whiteman:
> or R. Allan Whiteman, Esq.

Dentist

Jacquline Lyster, D.D.S.
(Office Address) or
Dr. Jacquline Lyster
(Home Address)

> Dear Dr. Lyster:

A

Appendix — Forms of Address

Physician
Terry Thomlinson, M.D.
(Office Address) or
Dr. Terry Thomlinson
(Home Address)
Dear Dr. Thomlinson:

Veterinarian
Cathy Hines, D.V.M.
(Office Address) or
Dr. Cathy Hines

Dear Dr. Hines:

British Nobility

Baron
The Lord Swarthmore
Dear Lord Swarthmore:

Baroness
The Lady Swarthmore
Dear Lady Swarthmore:

Duke
The Duke of Marlington
Dear Duke:

Duchess
The Duchess of Marlington
Dear Duchess:

Duke's Younger Son
The Lord William Wymore
Dear Lord William:

Wife of Duke's Younger
The Lady William Wymore
Dear Lady William:

Duke's Daughter
> The Lady Regina Wymore
>> Dear Lady Regina:

Earl
> The Earl of Tropingham
>> Dear Lord Cresswell:

Earl's Wife
> The Countess of Tropingham
>> Dear Lady Cresswell:

Knight
> Sir Reginald Williams
>> Dear Sir Reginald:

Marquess
> The Marquess of Cullertshire
>> Dear Lord Ranson:

Marchioness
> The Marchioness of Cullertshire
>> Dear Lady Ranson:

Viscount
> The Viscount Lindsay
>> Dear Lord Lindsay:

Viscountess
> The Viscountess Lindsay
>> Dear Lady Lindsay:

A

Notes

Notes

Notes

Notes

OTHER BOOKS FROM NATIONAL SEMINARS PUBLICATIONS

DESKTOP HANDBOOKS

	Item #	Title
LEADERSHIP	410	The Supervisor's Handbook, Revised and Expanded
	458	Positive Performance Management: *A Guide to Win-Win Reviews*
	459	Techniques of Successful Delegation
	463	Powerful Leadership Skills for Women
	494	Team-Building
	495	How to Manage Conflict
COMMUNICATION	413	Dynamic Communication Skills for Women
	414	The Write Stuff: *A Style Manual for Effective Business Writing*
	442	Assertiveness: *Get What You Want Without Being Pushy*
	460	Techniques to Improve Your Writing Skills
	461	Powerful Presentation Skills
	482	Techniques of Effective Telephone Communication
	485	Personal Negotiating Skills
	488	Customer Service: *The Key to Winning Lifetime Customers*
	498	How to Manage Your Boss
PRODUCTIVITY	411	Getting Things Done: *An Achiever's Guide to Time Management*
	468	Understanding the Bottom Line: *Finance for the Non-financial Manager*
	483	Successful Sales Strategies: A Woman's Perspective
	489	Doing Business Over the Phone: *Telemarketing for the 90s*
	496	Motivation & Goal-Setting: *The Keys to Achieving Success*
LIFESTYLE	415	Balancing Career & Family: *Overcoming the Superwoman Syndrome*
	416	Real Men Don't Vacuum
	484	The Stress Management Handbook
	486	Parenting: *Ward & June Don't Live Here Anymore*
	487	How to Get the Job You Want

BUSINESS USER'S MANUALS

Item #	Title
449	***Business Letters for Busy People,*** by Jim Dugger
451	***Think Like a Manager,*** by Roger Fritz

National Seminars Publications
6901 W. 63rd Street • P.O. Box 2949 • Shawnee Mission, Ks. 66201-1349
VIP #705-10449-091

Wait, There's More!

National Seminars Publications offers a complete line of career-development and self-improvement products designed to help you reach your career and personal goals. And every one of these products carries an unconditional guarantee of satisfaction. Just a small sample of the resources available:

AUDIOCASSETTE ALBUMS:

Item #	Title
116	**Powerful Business Writing Skills** - learn the most important skill for your career advancement on this six-cassette album.
199	**Becoming a Promotable Woman** - a six-cassette album, workbook and 500-page bestseller for women on the way up.
119	**LifePlanning** - this life-changing six cassette album that shows you how to set goals and plan your future.
121	**How to Handle Difficult People** - a four-cassette album that helps you understand and deal effectively with difficult behavior.
124	**Powerful Presentation Skills** - this four-tape series teaches you how to make presentations like a professional every time.
811	**The Power of Effective Listening** - learn to communicate more effectively by mastering the skills of active listening with this four tape series.

VIDEOCASSETTE PACKAGES:

Each package comes with a copy of the bestselling book it's based on and an audiocassette of the program.

Item #	Title
639	**How to Supervise People** - Techniques for getting results through others including delegation, motivation, goal-setting and more.
640	**How to Get Things Done** - Strategies for getting the most out of each day. Accomplish more, worry less!
641	**The Write Stuff** - Techniques to make your business reports, memos and proposals more powerful, more effective and easier to write.

National Seminars Publications
6901 W. 63rd Street • P.O. Box 2949 • Shawnee Mission, Ks. 66201-1349
VIP #705-10449-091